Chasi...

2nd Edition

A Memoir about Growing Up with ADHD

By Tom Nardone

© Tom Nardone 2017

Foreword by

Alan P. Brown

For Alex D'Argenio

Alex, you are my youngest fan, and the bravest man I know.
You sir are also... my hero.

Tom

Foreword

It was at the age of 36 that the "light bulb" lit up for me. The one that lights up when you realize maybe you're not as stupid, irresponsible, lazy or hopeless as you thought. Because, it turns out, you'd been hobbled by an invisible burden, undiagnosed up until then: ADD/ADHD.

On the day of my diagnosis, I rejoiced and literally ran from the doctor's office to a book store to buy books on adult ADHD coping strategies. In a classic impulsive act of ADHD abandon, I bought about six books, none of which I ever read much of. I'd forgotten in my rejoicing that I suck at reading.

Having set the books aside to collect dust with all my other impulsive purchases of the written word, over the next few weeks I pieced back together the many elements of my life that were influenced by my undiagnosed ADHD: massive underachievement in school; alcohol and drug abuse. It all made sense now that the light bulb had been turned on.

The thing that makes Tom Nardone's book — which begins with his own heart-wrenching "light bulb story" -- so good, is the same thing that pulled me into his orbit some years ago by way of his blog posts: His unique brand of vulnerability and hilarity. There was nothing else like Tom's writing in the ADHD blogosphere. And he remains a one-of-a-kind voice of revelation-by-humor.

Fortunately for you, the reader, Tom has put forth here a string of great stories -- of alienation, failure, trouble too easily found -- that illuminate, entertain and teach through that unique voice. I know you'll love this book. My copy's collecting zero dust.

Alan P. Brown
Creator of ADDCrusher.com and host of CrusherTV.com

Introduction

I arrived at Advanced Dealer Concepts early one Monday morning. I had three job interviews, and this was the first of them. Shortly after entering the building, I met the lady who was to interview me. Her name was Jean. She was a nice lady and easy to talk to. She began to tell me what my responsibilities for the position would be and what would be expected of me. The position for which I was interviewing was Customer Service Representative. After my interview, Jean felt I would be better suited for the Customer Service Supervisor position. The name alone scared me. Even though I really needed a job at the time, I did not see myself being successful if I were tasked with being in charge. It was more responsibility than I believed I could handle. I had no interest in this, and I was certain there was a huge potential for disaster.

I had a couple of other interviews to go to later, so I did not feel the need to push for this job. I told Jean during the interview I had a real problem with organization, focus and remembering things. I explained, for these reasons, I would probably not be right for the job. In spite of my best efforts, I was unable to convince her of my incompetence. She said I would do just fine, so I agreed to work there.

After the interview, Jean introduced me to my coworkers. They seemed really great, too. I felt pressured into this job, but I decided if she wanted me this bad, I would do my best. I was very worried about complicating the lives of Jean and my coworkers. I knew this was a mistake, but they were in need of someone right away. I would just have to try to avoid the disappointment that was all but assured as a result of my being at the helm of this company's customer service department.

While Jean was my supervisor, this was only to be temporary until I got up to speed on how the company worked. I answered to her during this time, but I also answered to Chet Smith. Chet was a very successful and professional person. He was always busy, and he dressed very well. He was a nice guy, but I found myself intimidated by him. I suppose because Jean talked him up so much during the interview, I had inferred him to be some kind of celebrity. For whatever reason this made me nervous when I spoke to him.

The first few days were very rocky because, as I expected, I had difficulty learning how to do all the tasks expected of me. Jean had to go behind me making sure everything I did was correct. I could see she was busy all day doing her own job. It was awkward for me when I had to watch her do mine as well because I didn't listen to her when I should have been. After a while, things did level out a little, and I eventually understood most of my daily responsibilities. All except for one.

My main responsibility at ADC, was to make "shopper calls". Twice a month, I would make calls to the car dealerships who had been trained by our company and signed up for the call service. I would call into the sales department and pose as a prospective buyer. It was my job to evaluate the salesmen and record the audio of the calls. I would write up the evaluations and send them with a copy of the tape for the owner of the dealership to hear.

I sucked at making shopper calls. It was not a training issue at all. No matter how many times Jean or Chet worked with me, I could not seem to become proficient enough to be believable. Both of them listened with me to a few of my calls each day. We talked about all the things I did wrong as we identified my mistakes. This was the worst part of my day.

I hated these training sessions. It was not long before I hated making the calls. This attitude did not help me do them any better. I think the problem was I had no interest in cars nor did I have any knowledge of them either. I did not really make an honest attempt to learn either. I was rarely able to convince the salesmen I was a legitimate customer. They caught me all the time, and the salesmen would call me out on the spot.

They would say, as they laughed, "Oh, is this one of those ADC shopper calls?" They usually told their sales manager about it, who would then tell the dealer, who would then call Chet. The dealers were not very happy since they were paying for these calls to test and review the skills of their sales force. Most of the calls I made were not believable, so I guess I couldn't blame them for being angry about it.

I screwed these calls up daily in new and different ways. I called dealerships who only sold trucks asking about cars. I would mismatch car makes with the wrong models. "Uh, yes sir, I am calling about a new Chevrolet, Accord." The sales people would be a little puzzled at first, but once they realized it was me calling, everything made sense to them. Eventually almost all of the salesmen knew my voice.

In the middle of my opening, they would interrupt me and say, "How have you been, Tom?" Sometimes we would even chit-chat for a while. Twice, I forgot to turn off the tape recorder and accidentally sent the dealership a tape of his salesman and I having conversations exceeding twenty minutes.

Some of the salesmen who caught me were very smug about it. This really bothered me because I hated making the calls, and I had to listen to their smart-ass comments while I was trying to do my job. I had hoped the shopper calls would magically just go away or Chet would tell Jean to have somebody else do them. This was not going to happen. The shopper calls were my main job so I knew I would have to do something different with them if I was going to be convincing.

I thought about this for days, and finally I got the answer. I thought maybe, I would try making calls using various accents. I ran this by Chet, and he was willing to let me to try anything. My very first call revealed the flaw in my plan. My English accent was less than convincing. I started as a man with an English accent looking for a car. I actually thought it was going pretty well, but halfway through the call my accent had become Australian. I did not quit after the first screw-up. I tried these accents again and again.

It was the worst idea ever. Sometimes in the middle conversations, I got put on hold. While I was waiting, I forgot what accent I was using. I might start off English, but when they returned I was American. I could not do a Canadian accent, so I tried an Indian accent and when the person returned, my accent was Russian. The shopper calls were becoming a big joke at the car dealerships. Chet's conversations with angry dealers were at an all-time high, and I was the cause. As a result of all my mistakes, many of the dealers called and cancelled their service. They claimed we were only distracting their salesmen from doing what they were supposed to be doing. It was difficult to hear, but they were right. The calls I made had no value to the salespeople.

By this time, I hated more than just the shopper calls; I hated my job. I hated getting up to go to work. I hated the drive to this place, and I hated the smell inside the building. I associated all of these things with my own failure. Re-calls and training were taking up so much of my time, Jean was doing all of my other jobs. I think the only thing I ever consistently did right was make it to work every day on time. Chet and Jean really gave me every chance to learn what I needed to know. I could see this was not going to work.

I knew I was never going to understand how that place worked, but they were not convinced of this yet. I wanted to quit, but Chet and Jean were so nice to me and so positive. They spent so much time trying to help me. I could not bring myself to quit because I respected them both.

Even though I went in each day with an attitude I was going to turn things around, ten minutes into my day, one mistake would remind me of the reality. I did not like that place, and I could not get past my hatred for being there. I was irritated all day every day. All I ever thought about was what I was going to screw up that day and how long it was until it was time to leave. I knew, one way or the other, I would not be there much longer

My final act of incompetence was a fiasco on a grander scale than anyone believed me capable. This was my final encore at ADC. It was a busy week. Chet had two seminars back to back. He would be in Chicago one week and then in Los Angeles the following week. Jean was nervous because Chet would be gone for two weeks. She explained to me what I was to do, and she was clear about the most important thing. She trusted me to ship all of the training materials to the locations where Chet was conducting his seminars. I remembered I had seen Jean doing this herself during my first week on the job.

It was simple, really. Jean had a list of what went where, and she even printed all of the labels for me. Chet had many different training programs. He was doing a different one in each of the two cities. I went by the list Jean had made and filled about fourteen boxes with forms, cassette tapes and workbooks. I managed to do all of this correctly. Jean came in to check on me and told me I was doing a great job. She even commented, "You are very methodical, Tom." I was thrilled she thought so. I was so happy I had pleased her and done a good job on something so important. She would not have been so impressed with me if she noticed I mixed up the labels on the boxes for both cities.

Yes, I did the unthinkable. I sent all of the Los Angeles materials to Chicago and all of the Chicago materials to Los Angeles.

Chet was enraged. He called Jean about this early Monday morning. She had a defeated look on her face when she mentioned it to me. I didn't know how to respond. I offered to quit, but she said it was not necessary. I did not expect I would get the same answer from Chet. It was a scary couple of weeks as the day of Chet's return drew closer. I was not looking forward to facing him.

For two weeks, the silence in the office was as that of a funeral or a wake. The weekend before he returned was a long and terrible one. I knew as soon as Monday morning came, I would have to face Chet, and I would have to answer for what I had done. I knew termination was inevitable. On Sunday, I bought a newspaper and began looking at jobs just as I had done so many times before. I set up some interviews for Monday late in the afternoon. I thought it would be best to give Chet ample time to come in, get settled, yell at me for as long as he felt he needed to and ultimately fire me.

When I arrived on Monday, Jean was already there. It was an hour before Chet would arrive. I hoped he would take the day off, or maybe he would find something funny about the whole thing. An hour later, I was making my shopper calls as I always did in the morning. As I got off a call, I became aware of Chet when he slammed his hand down on my desk. He said, "Pack it up! You are done here!"

I hoped I could just pack up my personal belongings and walk out to my car and go home without any further communication. I gathered my stuff quietly, and started toward the door. Chet came back to speak to me. He had calmed down a bit and apologized. He said, "Tom, can you come into my office for a minute?"

I said, "Sure, Chet." I walked into his office. He pointed to the chair in front of his desk and told me to close the door. I sat down wondering why he could possibly want to hear anything I had to say.

Chet began by apologizing to me for slamming down his hand on my desk earlier. Then he said, "Tom, is there anything you think of we can do to help you and prevent these daily problems from happening?"

I said, "No, sir." I went on to explain to Chet these problems were the story of my life, and I knew this would happen. I told him I explained to Jean I wasn't right for this job when she hired me. I told Chet I fully expected all of this to happen. He asked if I knew what the problem was. I told him I had no explanation to offer him. It was just the way things were for me.

Chet's next words were a revelation to me. Chet said, "Tom, I know this has been happening to you your whole life. Believe me I do. Have you ever heard of something called ADHD? It stands for Attention Deficit Hyperactivity Disorder?"

I told him I had not. He explained the signs and symptoms to me. As he spoke to me, I could not believe how many things he knew about me. Then, he explained someone very close to him also suffered with this. He told me this person had the exact same problems he saw me having. He shared the specific occurrences and problems this person had experienced in school. We talked for over an hour.

When we finished, I shook his hand, and he wished me well. I left the building that morning, and I felt great. I wasn't angry or sad. I was intrigued and curious. I was encouraged by the things he had explained to me. I went to my other interviews and then to a bookstore. I bought a book about ADHD. I couldn't believe what I was reading. I read what the symptoms of Attention Deficit Hyperactivity Disorder were. The more I read, the better I felt. I didn't read the whole book. I just read about the symptoms. I read them repeatedly over the weeks that followed. The veil had been lifted. At last, I knew the reason for all the pain and frustration I had gone through in my life. I had wondered for years what it was about me and why I was so different from others.

I learned what caused me to be the one explaining why I could not do certain things others seemed to do so effortlessly. I learned there was a reason I had trouble concentrating and paying attention to instructions I was given. There was a reason I hopped from job to job and got fired so often. There was a reason I had such a tough time in school.

Almost every problem I had ever faced was somehow in this book. I always hoped there was an explanation for the things I did, but I did not know other people were suffering with them, too. The problems I experienced while I worked for Chet Smith were the same problems I had struggled with for most of my life. I always started out trying to please people. Sooner or later my efforts served only to see them disappointed. I now had answers to so many of the questions about my life. I believed things did not have to be this way anymore, and life could be better for me. Maybe, things were about to change.

Chet Smith is the finest human being for whom I have ever worked. I cost him thousands of dollars. I tarnished his reputation and made him look stupid. Nobody would have blamed him for just firing me the minute he saw me that morning. In spite of all the embarrassment, money, time and energy I cost him, he cared enough about me to steer me in a direction that could help me and would ultimately change the course of my life. He told me what no one else ever had.

Hello, friends. I am Tom Nardone, and up to this point, I had gone my entire life not knowing why so many things were so difficult for me. I had never heard of anything called ADHD. I thought I would somehow be able to improve my life because I identified the problem. I was wrong. It would be another five years before I got a diagnosis from a doctor or any type of treatment.

I have made some very poor decisions in my life. I do not ask for your sympathy. My life is the result of the choices I have made. In the end, we play the hand we are dealt. We are responsible for the people we become, and the lives we make for ourselves whether we are ADHD or not.

This is not a "how to" manual or an outline for how people should deal with their ADHD or the problems it presents. These are the things I went through and the choices I made. I am aware, some of the choices I made were not appropriate or warranted. It is not my intention to suggest all people who are ADHD resort to the measures or form the same opinions I have.

I chose to share stories from the most difficult times in my life. I have done so to give you, the reader, a front row seat and a clear picture of the life of a person living with ADHD. I spared no words in sharing my experiences or the sum of them. This was not easy for me to do, and I struggled with deciding what stories would and would not go into it.

While most of the stories I remember vividly, I have little memory of the stories about the early years of my life. I had to depend on members of my family and their account of them to fill in the gaps. While much of what you read will be entertaining and funny, it was nonetheless my reality at the time. I think you will laugh through much of this, and I invite you to do so at my expense.

I write this to the non-ADHD spouses and significant others. There are many people with ADHD in relationships and marriages who are unable to articulate what being ADHD really means. It is my hope you will read and understand what it might have been like for your loved one to deal with challenges they had and may still face today.

I write this to the moms and dads of children with ADHD. I want you to understand the problems and challenges your child is facing are very real to them. As parents we want what is best for our kids. It is a difficult thing for a child to articulate the reasons why their work performance is poor in school or around the house. I hope my experiences will give you some insight as to what they might be up against.

I write this to teachers of students who are ADHD who are not sure why they seemingly set themselves up for failure each day. I want you to see there are things going on in their lives besides school that have a direct effect on their ability to care about what you ask of them in your classroom.

Most of all, I write this to the ADHD community. You who are ADHD; I want you all to see you are not alone. Many of the things you went through are the same thing I and many others have been through or are going through. It is my hope you will find my adventures to be relatable and inspiring.

I grew up in a world I did not understand and a world that seemed to make no attempt to understand me. This is the story of me and the architects who unknowingly built me. I am Tom Nardone. I am ADHD.

Welcome to my show.

Chapter 1

My father, Tom Nardone, Sr. was a wonderful man and a great storyteller. His favorite thing in the world to talk about was the things my brothers and I did when we were children. He told these stories to us often.

One of my father's favorite stories happened in 1974. My parents, Tom and Susan Nardone, were trying to sell a car. It was a yellow 1967 Toyota Celica. They were desperately in need of money. My father had been keeping it washed and waxed for weeks, just in case someone called about it. My dad finally received a call from a man who wanted the car and agreed to buy it at my father's asking price of $300. My dad immediately ran out of the house and told my mother. He and my mom ran back in the house, leaving me outside. My mother and I had been playing together in our front yard. When they left me alone, I started throwing small rocks across the yard. I waited and waited for them to come back outside, but I eventually got bored, so I had to think of something else to do.

Mom had been teaching me how to write my name. She had even told me, since I had the same name as my Dad, I would also be able to write his name. I always desired the approval of my father. I wanted my dad to know everything I did and to hear him say he was proud of me. I would even ask him sometimes, "Daddy, are you proud of me?" I knew if I was able to show him how I could write the name we shared, he would be pleased with me. I decided I would do this while my dad was still inside and show him when he came back out.

I began looking for something to write on, but there was no paper or flat surface anywhere on which to write. It was then I saw the shiny yellow car in the driveway. I would simply just use one of my rocks and write on the trunk lid. I walked over to the car and climbed onto the trunk. With my rock I began to scratch the letters onto the unblemished surface of the trunk lid. T... o... m... m..., and then, it might as well have been the hand of God snatching me off the car and setting me gently to my feet on the driveway. It was not actually the hand of God. It was the hand of my father.

My father stood there, as he often did when anyone did something stupid. He stood there without a word. With his mouth open, he stared in amazement at what I had done. It was as if he were trying to accept this really happened. I was four and could not understand the gravity of my actions.

I thought he was staring at my name and was so pleased with the fact I could do it by myself, it rendered him speechless. I said "Dad, you did not let me finish. I still have to put the Y on the end."

Dad took this opportunity to break his silence and yelled out, "Susan!"

My mom came running outside. "Tommy, what are you yelling about?"

Dad just said, "Take him somewhere. Now!"

My mom saw the car and started asking questions, such as what happened, how did that happen and can it still be sold. Dad explained, in a heated tone, this was not the time for questions. Mom took me inside and told me to go to my room and to stay there.

My dad ran into the garage, got the car wax and started working on the trunk. I remember watching him through my bedroom window as he feverishly tried to wax away the scratches I had made. I knew then my dad was mad, and I knew it was because of what I had done. I knew he was not happy with me in spite of my best intentions. I began to cry because I disappointed my father. I disappointed my hero.

My dad was able to get almost all of the scratches buffed out. When the man and his friend arrived and met my father in the driveway, they all shook hands and said hello. The two men walked around the car nodding their heads and then one of them looked up and said, "Okay, $300 it is." As the man handed my dad the money, my dad shook his head and said he was sorry but he couldn't accept the $300 for the car. He explained to them what had happened moments before their arrival and walked them around to the back of the car. Dad showed them the almost invisible scratches I had put there with my rock.

The two men began laughing as they tried to make out my name through the layers of wax my father worked so hard to apply. They said, "Sir, even if those scratches were visible, this car is worth every bit of the $300 you are asking. Don't worry about it."

Through my bedroom window, I saw my dad waving at both cars as they drove off. He came inside, and I heard him go into his bedroom. I remember I did not want to look at my dad. I think I didn't want to see a close-up view of the anger on his face knowing I was the reason for it. It was a bit later when he knocked at my door. I jumped up quickly and opened it.

He had a sad and disappointed look on his face. But it was not in me he was disappointed. He walked into my room and told me in a soft voice to sit down. He sat on the floor right beside me and said, as he tried not to cry, "Tommy, I'm sorry I got mad at you out there. And I am sorry that I yelled at you." He asked me if I was all right.

I told him "Dad, I didn't mean to make you mad at me. I was trying to make you proud of me."

My father said, "I know Tommy. I am not mad at you." He calmly explained, as best as he could, what the problem was and told me everything turned out fine. He told me he knew what I was trying to do and why I did it. He had brought a piece of paper and a pencil. When he was finished talking with me, he handed it to me and asked if I would show him how I write our name. I was happy to do it for him.

I acknowledge perhaps this example alone might not be a telltale sign of childhood ADHD. I think any four-year-old child is capable of such an act. Every time I was present during my father telling this story, I would ask him why I did this. He always gave the same answer, "You wanted me to be proud of you." Both of my parents have spoken of this and agreed it was an obsession I had as a child to always be the center of attention. I always wanted people to be impressed with whatever I did or was doing. This was especially true when it came to my father.

I always had my own way of doing things and would often over-think them. I always wanted to help both of my parents as a child. I did not like to be left alone ever and could not stand to be the only one awake in the house. It was always my first order of business to wake up somebody the moment I got out of bed each morning. My mother told me a story of one of such a morning because I had no memory of it.

Mom was on a break from school, and she worked nights. I got up one morning before anybody else. I was bored and hungry. I wanted breakfast, and my mother, for some reason, decided to sleep a little later than usual this morning. I knocked on her door. She did not answer. I entered the room and walked over to her and shook her. She was tired from working the previous evening. I asked her to get up and fix my breakfast. She said, "Okay, Tommy, I'm getting up. Go in the den, and I'll be right there." I left, and mom fell back asleep. I woke her up a second time. She said, "Okay, Tommy, I'm getting up. Go in the den, and I'll be right there." I left and mom fell back asleep, again. I would have to wake her a third time.

I was going to help her because I knew she was tired. I did the only thing I knew how to do in the process of cooking a pot roast. I went into the

16

kitchen and got a chair and pushed it in front of the refrigerator. I climbed up onto the chair, opened the freezer door and pulled out a frozen, uncooked pot roast. I carried this heavy piece of frozen meat into her bedroom and threw it into the bed with her. This startled her, but then she began to laugh. She got out of the bed and went into the kitchen to make my breakfast.

I spent the whole day trying to get her to play with me. I would run around the house dropping toys wherever I was standing when I saw another toy. Sometimes I was rough with my toys, and they would break. I never cared or asked for them to be fixed. I simply moved on to the next toy. This went on all day. My mother could not clean as fast as I could mess up. I was constantly opening doors and boxes and making messes from one end of the house to the other.

I was non-stop, and all day long asking questions or asking if I could help her. She could not believe all the questions I asked, and I was in need of constant attention all day long. The only time she got to do anything for herself was during my naps, which were not often.

Mom and Dad realized I needed something to do with my time. I was driving my mother insane, and her patience was wearing thin. My mother loved spending time with me all day, but she was getting nothing done around the house. My parents looked into many activities searching for something I could do, but I was too young for most of them. Finally, they found something which would give my dad his favorite story to tell about my childhood.

There was a baseball park down the street from our house. My parents signed me up for T-Ball. I was younger than the average player, but they were happy to find something to occupy some of my time and energy. At first, I was very excited about it. All I talked about was the uniform I would get to wear. I was finally going to do something with kids my own age. I was happy I was going to have all those people watching me. The first thing I ever learned about T-ball was I did not know how to play T-ball. I believe the reason for this was I was not interested in it. I just liked the idea of wearing my uniform each week and going to the games and practices. I talked often of the uniform and being a part of a team, but I didn't talk much about playing T-ball. I talked about the uniform and going to the games. Never about the game itself. T-ball just gave me somewhere to go and something to do.

I was always in the outfield when our team wasn't at bat. I had no idea how to play this game. I used to ask my coach, "Do I have to go in the outfield today?" I told my coach, I just wanted to hit, so could I just sit on the bench and watch the game until it was my turn at bat? He never once granted that request.

I did not understand what the purpose of standing out there was. I didn't know I was supposed to try to get the ball when it came near me. If I did get it, I didn't have a clue what to do with it. When the ball did come to me, I would walk over and hand it to somebody who did know while the other team ran the bases. My father was no sports enthusiast, but he explained to me many times what to do when I got the ball. I rarely listened.

I paid absolutely no attention to the game. I was unable to follow it. I did not even know or care if we won, lost or tied. I had to ask my coach at the end of each game whether we won or lost. The only reason I asked was for when I got home and my parents would ask, "Did you win, Tommy?" Many times, I just forgot to ask the coach and had no idea how we did.

My coach used to yell at me because I would get tired of standing out there during practice and at the games. I would take my glove off and sit on it. Sometimes, I would sit with my back to the infield. My coach would go crazy because I was too far away to hear him yell. He had to come out onto the field to get my attention. Everybody would wait while he walked out there and asked me to stand up and pay attention.

My dad worked three jobs and could not make it for most of my games, but he did go to at least one game I remember. I was excited when Dad told me he was going to my next game. He would never forget the first game he saw me play. On the day of the game, both my parents and I went to the park. I did not want to embarrass them, so I made sure I did not sit down on my glove for this game.

I did, however, find another way to shame myself and my family in front of all the other parents and spectators on this fine Saturday afternoon. As usual, I was in the outfield, and, as usual, I got very bored. I knew I could not sit on my glove, so I would just have to deal with it. Everything was going okay until I looked up in the air and saw a most remarkable site. Unfortunately, this was far more interesting than the ball game.

It was absolutely beautiful. I watched as it soared through the air. It was a giant diamond-shaped object with a long tail of shiny ribbons. I was fascinated as I watched it fly through the air; up and down and side-to-side. It would dive and go plummeting toward the earth and then, just as quickly, it would shoot back up into the air going higher and higher. I was mesmerized. I could not take my eyes off it. To most people this was just a kite, but to me, it was something amazing.

I stared at this kite for a long time. I kept wondering what it would do next. I thought how wonderful it would be to be flying this kite instead of standing out on this stupid hot baseball field doing nothing. As I stood looking to the sky, time stood still. There was no game. There was no coach. There was no earth. The only thing in the world of whose existence I was conscious was this beautiful kite. I was in "la la land", and I did not want to leave. I could have watched that kite fly around for hours, and I would have never complained.

While deep into my kite fantasy world, I saw a shadow unexpectedly cast over me. I turned toward this impending disturbance and saw it was my coach. He was kind enough to walk all the way out to the outfield in the middle of the game and bring me up to speed on some exciting developments in the game that took place while I was away. Apparently, while I was in my own little land of kites and ribbons, the game had taken a significant turn. The coach explained to me the other team managed not only to load the bases, but also to hit a grand slam home run. The tragic part of this was that ball rolled on the ground right between my feet and stopped only a short distance beyond me. I was standing there completely unaware any of this had happened.

After the coach was finished giving me the game highlights, I explained very remorsefully, "Coach, I'm sorry I was watching that kite fly over there. I did not mean to make you mad at me. But keep watching, Coach, in a second, it's really gonna do something cool."

My coach in a very irritated voice said, "Well, tell me something, Nardone. Do you want to play baseball? Or do you wanna go fly a kite?" Without another word to the coach I threw my glove down and ran all the way to the backstop.

There, I located my father in the crowd and said as loudly as I could, "Dad, the coach said it was okay if we left to go fly a kite!" The laughter of everyone in the stands was uncontrollable and went on for minutes. The coach benched me for the remainder of the game. I don't imagine the team was too unhappy about this.

My dad went to speak to my coach after the game. "Coach? My name is Tom Nardone. I am Tommy's father." The coach was pleased to meet him and shook his hand.

"Nice to meet you. What can I do for you, Mr. Nardone?"

"How is Tommy doing on this team? And please sir, tell me the truth. It's okay." The coach stopped what he was doing and looked at my dad. "Well, as you could probably see today, Tommy is not the best player we have on this team." My dad began to speak, but the coach interrupted him to say, "But he is the most well-mannered and respectful kid that I have ever coached in 15 years." My father could not have been more pleased. My dad did not care if I was any good at T-ball. He was proud of me in spite of my performance. He was proud I was just a good kid.

He walked over to my mother and me and put his arm around me. I just kept asking, "Are you proud of me, Dad?"

My dad just looked at me and said, "You better believe I am, Tommy."

As funny as this story is today, it was in no way what I had planned. I was in the outfield during a game in front of my father and many other people who were watching and expecting me to do my job. I went out there with my mind made up not to disappoint anyone. All it took to distract me was a kite. I couldn't hear the crowd yelling as runners loaded the bases. I did not notice a baseball roll right between my feet. I did not even notice my own team members running by me to get the ball. I didn't see. I saw nothing except that amazing kite that held my attention hostage. All I saw was a kite.

This fiasco did not happen because no one took time to teach me the game. My father and my coach spent time teaching me what to do. My father told me on the few practices he witnessed he always wondered why the coach was standing right next to me for the entire practice. I not only was taught, but a special interest was also taken in my T-ball education. Dad would explain years later, I was excited to go play until it was time to play, and then I just got bored and did not pay attention. I just had no interest in it.

I believe this is my earliest memory of what we all understand today as ADHD. All I wanted out of T-ball was for my mom and dad to cheer for me as I ran around the bases. I wanted them to jump up and yell, just as the other parents did when their sons played well. I desperately wanted the approval of my father. So, for what possible reason did I do such a thing? The kite was not as important as my mother or my father. At least not until I saw it. I saw the kite, and the rest of the world vanished. I did not intentionally tune the game out. I just saw a kite, and for a few moments the game, my coach and my parents were nonexistent.

The point of this is: in spite of a need I had and any effort I made to play well, I was unsuccessful, and it was because of my attention to a kite flying through the air. I did not decide I no longer cared what my dad or my coach thought. I did not decide to check out of the game. I had every intention of paying attention and staying focused during the game for the sake of the people who loved me. I never decided I did not care about them. I only realized it had happened when it was too late. It just came as a big surprise to me.

This kite was the first of many kites I would see in my life. Many things like this kite distracted, detoured or stole my focus and my attention from what my purpose was supposed to be. My kites appeared in many forms. They appeared as anything I happened to see or think about. They were things I saw, things I imagined, things I was excited about or things that scared me.

My father never left a doubt in my mind he loved me. He was a very reasonable man. He always preferred talking with me instead of shouting at me. Unfortunately for him and for me, shouting was the only way I could hear him. Shouting was the only way he could get my attention most of the time. There were two cardinal rules my father had for me and for my brothers while we were growing up. My father absolutely required two things of us. There was never a discussion about these two things. They were, as he would say, taboo. We were never to be disrespectful to an adult, particularly my mother, and to never touch his tools. My father talked about these things constantly, but he talked about his tools the most.

Anytime I saw my dad using his tools, I would ask him questions about what he was doing. He would answer my questions until I irritated him to the point he would say, "Tommy, go inside and pester your mother. She isn't doing a damn thing today." On the occasions I managed to stay in his presence, he would always take the opportunity to remind me his tools were never to be touched. I don't think there was ever anything about which he was clearer than he was about his tools.

In spite of my father's clarity and in spite of how many times he calmly explained to me the rules of his tools, it wasn't enough to penetrate my thick skull. I was home one day, and Mom was taking a nap with my brothers before she had to go to work. Dad was not home from work yet. I was bored, so I went into Dad's workshop to see if I could find something to do. As soon as I entered his shop, I saw those tools hanging on the wall so neatly.

I wondered what it was like to use the tools my father used. I knew I was never to touch them. I knew I needed to put them back exactly how I found them. It was only one hammer and two screwdrivers. I went outside, but I had nothing to build or fix. I began pounding a screwdriver into the ground with the hammer. I took the next screwdriver to see if I could pound it in on top of the previous one to send them deep into the dirt in the backyard. I went back for more screwdrivers, and kept going back in for more screwdrivers until they were all gone. Of course, me being me, I left the hammer on the ground where I finished using it. I went back inside thinking nothing of what I had done and just found something else to get into. I completely forgot the consequences of what I had done.

I did not think about this again until a few days later. Saturday came, and my father was working on something and needed a screwdriver. Dad went into his shop to get one and quickly realized they were all gone. He kept them displayed on the wall very neatly. He had the big ones on the far left, and they got smaller toward the right side. He must have had thirty screwdrivers, but every single one was missing. Dad couldn't believe what he was not seeing. He came to me and calmly asked me if I took his screwdrivers. I did not ever lie to my father, so I told him, "Yes, sir." He, in a less calm manner, asked me if I knew the rule about touching his tools, and I said, "Yes, sir." He asked me where they were, and I told him they were in the yard. He immediately asked me to show him. I took him outside, pointed at the ground and said while I was crying, "They are all right there, Dad."

My father, who was very irritated at this point, said, "Tommy, I don't see them. Where in the hell are they, son?" I explained to him they were in the ground. My dad did not understand. He said, "Tommy, son, you are not making any damn sense. Now, where are my screwdrivers, and how did they get there?" I managed to stop crying long enough to explain what I had done. He lost it. He couldn't believe I would have done something so ridiculous.

Dad looked at me angrily and said, "Come here, now!" We went into his shop, and he grabbed a log-splitting wedge that was made of solid steel. I had already begun to cry again as he looked at me and said at the top of his lungs, "Do you know what my father would have done if I had so much as put one of my hands on his tools?" I fearfully shook my head. He then shouted, "He would have taken my hand and put it on this table and smashed it as hard as he could!" For effect, when he said the word smashed, he hit his workbench as hard as he could with the steel log wedge he was holding. It was very loud, and it really scared me.

I don't want you to think my father tyrant. He knew me very well, and he was forever telling me about touching his tools. He learned over the course of many similar instances if he did not make a big show for me, I would never hear him. He was right. I would have taken his tools again and again. Thanks to his psychotic display of anger, his tools were now safe from my curiosity, and I never touched them again. He grounded me for a month, and when my dad grounded me for a month, he meant it. I remained a prisoner for a month.

I can't recall how many times I sat in my room crying not because I was grounded, but because, once again, I had disappointed the man who loved me more than anyone else in the world. I couldn't believe I had taken my dad's tools and treated them this way. Why would I have caused this man to be so angry with me? I felt like I had betrayed him and stolen from him. I could not understand why I would have done this.

This was one of Dad's two commandments. He made this clear to me on many occasions. I was bored and had nothing to do, so this act of stupidity was all I could come up with. I imagine the only thing I thought of as I drove those screwdrivers into the ground was I had finally found something to do to entertain myself. I would have not even considered it if I had thought about it. I knew better than to ever touch Dad's tools. I didn't even make an effort to conceal it. This kite manifested itself in the form of my own curiosity to know what it was like to use the tools belonging to my hero.

Incidents such as these were common. I was not a rebellious child. I had never even so much as back-talked my mother or father. They made the rules clear to me, but the things I saw as a small child were of great interest to me. When they took over, they were greater than my parents' commands.

With children who have ADHD, it is as if the sound of their own thoughts are louder than anyone or anything else in their lives. Many don't ignore authority intentionally for the most part, but when they do get focused on something, it is difficult to break them free. This makes it impossible for them to comprehend instructions or commands. The kite they are figuratively staring at becomes the real world to them for that moment.

My mother told me I was a happy child most days, aside from a number of incidents around the house for which I got in trouble. She says I loved waking up every morning and having an adventure. She also tells me I was very excited about starting school, and I could not wait to begin and meet other kids and make friends. I was asking her questions everyday about the kids, the teachers, recess and lunch. I was so excited and so curious.

My curiosity did not last long. I learned quick what was to be the next thirteen years of my life. I say from my heart, in the darkest hours of my youth, I did not have the capacity to understand or the imagination to conceive of such a cold and malicious place. School was the place where I first asked myself the question I would be asking for the next ten years of my life: Why does everybody hate me?

Chapter 2

I have no memory of kindergarten. My mother tells me I enjoyed it and went through it with only a few hiccups, but there were no real problems. I don't know what kids in kindergarten do today, but my kindergarten was more of an art class than anything else. I used to get excited to come home and show her the things I made or what I had learned each day.

The following year, I attended Cartersville Elementary School. I began the first grade, but a few weeks into it, my teacher decided I was not ready. They placed me into what they called "Readiness". The main reason was because I would cry while I was at school for no apparent reason. This would happen two or three times per week. No one, myself included, could figure out why I was crying. They would ask me if I was sick or was it something at home, but it wasn't any of those things. The only answer I ever offered was, "I don't know."

I remember my readiness teacher well. Her name was Ms. Lee, and she was an amazing lady. Ms. Lee was very nice to me, and I really liked to listen to her talk. I thought she was pretty, and I enjoyed it very much when she spoke to me. She had such a pleasant voice. When I cried in her class she took me by the hand, and we left the room to go into the hallway. She cried as she pleaded with me. "Tommy, please. I want to help you, but you have got to tell me what is wrong."

I only answered, "I don't know."

In spite of it all, I did go on to the first grade the following year where I had a lady who was not nearly as sweet as Ms. Lee. Her name was Mrs. Sweeney. The first grade was where my problems began. I was small for my age, but other than the occasional crying in class I didn't know what made me so different from the rest of the kids. Whatever it was, my classmates did not like it, and they took great pride and pleasure making things difficult for me.

The worst part was I was constantly picked on and made fun of by the other students. They would make fun of my name, my clothes, my hair, my parents, what I brought to school for lunch or anything else they believed would upset me. They found it particularly amusing when one of them could get me to cry. This seemed to be a source of entertainment for them. It wasn't very hard to do since there was a chance I would just start crying anyway for no reason.

I don't know why they took this much pleasure in making me feel bad. All I wanted to do was to be nice to people and make friends. I did not want to fight or argue, and I had no ill feelings toward anybody. In my life, up to this point, nobody ever treated me this way. I hadn't a clue from where this was coming. I would have understood if the members of my T-ball team gave me a hard time. I jammed the whole team up at every game we played, but these people didn't even know me. I tried to get to know them, but they just had no interest in talking to me unless it was in the form of ridicule.

The playground was the worst place for this. Recess was the time I looked forward to the least. Many of these kids wanted to fight me. They would constantly hit me in the arm or the chest and try to provoke me. I remember asking my teacher if I could do extra work in the library instead of going outside for recess. She would ask why, and I lied and told her I did not want to be outside. She always said, "No!" I hated her for that. I never did tell my parents about any of this. I thought it would hurt them too much to hear it, and I would end up feeling worse. I just did not want to add to their trouble. I suppose I could have enjoyed recess, but every time I would get on a swing or the slide, the other kids would come over and make things difficult for me until I left. I eventually ended up just sitting on the ground near the teacher until it was time to go inside.

I never stood up for myself. I didn't know how because there had never been a need for it. I just took it day after day. It got to the point where I dreaded going to school. It was not long until I hated school. There was no more excitement or enthusiasm left in me for school. I didn't just hate school; I hated all the things relating to school. I hated the clock on the wall at home I looked at to know when to leave in the morning to catch the bus. I hated the bus I rode because it took me to the school. I hated every brick in the building. I hated the smell of that place as I entered the building. I felt anger toward my parents for making me go to that place. I cried in my bed at night as I thought about the day that would follow. I would have done anything to avoid going to school.

There was only one part I didn't hate. Art class was great. I always looked forward to it because it afforded me a measure of peace. I guess the other kids were too preoccupied with their own projects to worry about bothering me. Once in art class, we had a project where we took a piece of construction paper and wrote our names on it with glue. Before the glue dried, we sprinkled glitter on it to make a shiny, glittery image of our name. Somehow, mine came out better than most of the other kids, and my art teacher was very pleased. She held it up for the whole class to see. The class seemed impressed. I was proud for a brief moment. I kept reliving this moment in my head over and over.

A couple of days later, we had an assignment in Mrs. Sweeney's class. She wrote three sentences on the board, and we were to copy them. I carefully copied the sentences and was about to turn in my assignment. Then, I remembered how excited my art teacher was about my art project earlier in the week. Mrs. Sweeney was a mean old bat, and I never got the sense she liked me, but I really wanted this to change. I wanted her to be pleased with me, and I had a great idea for doing this.

I got out my art supplies and wrote my name on my classwork with my glue, just as I had done in art class. I sprinkled the glitter on the glue just as I had done in art class. I remember the kid sitting next to me saying, "I wouldn't do that." I did not care what anyone else thought. I was convinced she would be as thrilled as my art teacher was. I knew Mrs. Sweeney would be impressed. I was unable to let the glue dry since I had to turn my work in before the day ended. When the bell rang, I got up and carefully turned in my assignment. The rest of the class, who had not finished, turned their work in on their way out of the classroom. They placed their papers in the basket right on top of mine. The day ended, and we all went to our buses.

I could not wait to see Mrs. Sweeney's reaction to my beautifully crafted name at the top of my classwork. The next day at school, Mrs. Sweeney came to me the moment she saw me and took me by my arm. All she said as she grabbed me was, "Tommy Nardone, you come with me now!" We quickly walked out of the classroom. She was furious about something, and I had no idea what it was. The whole class was excited and happy about the idea of me being in trouble. I had no idea where Mrs. Sweeney was taking me or why. When got to the janitor's closet, we entered it, and she slammed the door.

She asked me, "Tommy Nardone, did you pour glue all over the classwork assignments yesterday?" Apparently, my classwork/art project idea did not impress her in the way I had hoped it would. It had caused all of the other papers to stick together in a big gluey mess. Seeing yet another one of my bright ideas fail and cause my teacher a great deal of grief was not what I needed that morning. So, I did what I always did when this happened; I cried. I explained to her I just wanted her to be proud of me for making my name look nice for my classwork assignment. I explained how I did this in art class, and I wanted her to be as happy as the art teacher was.

She must have believed me because she actually began to laugh hysterically as she gave me a hug and apologized for getting mad at me and thinking I was causing trouble. This is the only time I think I ever saw her smile. I thought of all the stupid and unimportant things that made her angry, but this disaster was somehow deserving of not just leniency but also a hug.

Unfortunately this debacle, just as so many others before it, became a source of fuel for the class to tease me and tell me how stupid I was. They got plenty of mileage out of it. All of the kids in the class decided to capitalize on this incident. "Tommy, make sure you don't put glue all over my classwork this time." Or "Hey Tommy, if you need to write your name on your paper, use a pencil." It became a race to see who could say it first after each assignment we were given. The kids seemed to enjoy having the other students thinking they were funny or clever. I guess this was one of the better ways they could demonstrate to the rest of the class how smart they could be. It seemed to me like a contest to see who could be the biggest asshole.

In first grade, I was just "that kid", and I don't remember anyone else in the class being treated the way I was treated. Every now and then, I saw a glimmer of hope, when the attention would turn to someone else. Somebody else would finally do something stupid, and then the class would be all over him or her for a change.

Although it was a rare occurrence when this happened, I had no interest in teasing them along with the class. I would usually try to say something nice to them. I was all too familiar with how this type of meanness felt. I thought if the class was harassing them then maybe I could be friends with them. It never quite happened that way. The minute I tried to say a kind word, they would lash back at me loudly where the whole class could hear them. Magically, they would almost immediately regain their status in the Thank God I am not Tom Nardone Club and reestablish their credibility with the other classmates as a fellow asshole.

My bus was the very first to arrive at the school, so I got to school earlier than the rest of the kids in my class did. I was the first one into the classroom each morning. I would sit at my desk and watch as all of the students enter. I remember watching the door each morning as I wished for certain students to be absent, so I could have some hope of peace for the day.

One morning as I was walking to my classroom, I passed by the lunchroom, looked inside and saw the big black man who worked as a janitor. He politely said, "Good morning, little man," and then he waved at me. All of the kids in my class made fun of him because he was black and because he was a janitor. I stopped and decided to introduce myself to him. After all, we had something in common: My class did not like him either.

When I entered the lunchroom, I saw the janitor setting up the chairs in the cafeteria. I walked up to him, introduced myself and asked his name. He told me his name was Melvin. I took the opportunity to ask him questions about what he was doing and why. He was happy to explain it all to me. I liked him immediately, and I made visiting Melvin a regular part of my morning routine. He eventually let me help him set up the chairs in the lunchroom, and every morning after we were finished he would sit with me and talk as we ate a piece of cake or whatever was on the dessert menu for the day. The class made fun of me for befriending Melvin. This didn't matter to me. I loved Melvin, and I was used to the class's callous remarks. I did not see anything wrong with being black or being a janitor.

During a conversation with Melvin, I told him how the class treated me. I told him about all of the awful things my fellow students did and said to me. Melvin asked me why I would let them do this. He didn't like it when I said, "I don't know." He told me I needed to stand up for myself, but he offered no further explanation. I was angry at Melvin for not explaining to me how to stand up for myself.

It became clear to me at some point: Nothing I could do was ever going to win the hearts and minds of my class. I just took it and took it and never retaliated. I took it every day, all day, and did nothing about it. I took it until the day I decided I was tired of taking it. I decided maybe I should give something back to those little bastards who had given me so much. One day, I did get pushed too far.

There was this particularly evil kid in my class named Roman. I avoided him at all costs. Roman was normally the ringleader for the class's ridicule toward me. Roman was the kid all the other kids feared. He loved to steer the focus toward me whenever possible. Every time I thought I might go a full day without any drama, Roman was sure to get something started. He was the first person I ever hated.

One morning I was in the bathroom standing at the urinal adjacent to the first stall. Someone entered the restroom, went to the first stall and began to pee. As soon as they began to pee their aim was adjusted at my left shoe. I quickly move my foot out of the stream of piss. This infuriated me. I did not even know who did it because I couldn't see them through the partition. I went around to the stall door to see who

29

had done this. Wouldn't you know it was that white-trash, redneck, troublemaker himself? Roman began to laugh the minute we made eye contact. He couldn't wait to get back to the class room so he could tell all his friends what he had done.

I walked around all day listening to the sound of my shoe he saturated with his piss. My left shoe made a squishy noise everywhere we went. Roman cashed in huge on his little stunt. He was bragging all day to the entire class about what he had done. The class spent the rest of the day asking me "Hey, Tommy, why is your shoe all wet?" or "Does anyone hear that noise?" or "Someone smells like pee. Tommy, is it you?" My first thought was to go to the teacher, but I was sure she would not care. Mrs. Sweeney was pretty vocal about kids telling on other kids. She called them "tattletales".

I thought all day about the problems I had to deal with every day from my classmates. I spent the whole school year taking a daily dose of their bullying and ridicule. I decided enough is enough. I decided I was going to stand up for myself and staying out of trouble wasn't worth being peed on. I decided as long as I was going to get myself into trouble with my parents and teachers, I was going to make sure Roman gave me my money's worth.

It was near the end of the day, and Roman sneaked out of class to use the bathroom. As soon as he left, I got up and asked for permission to use the bathroom. Mrs. Sweeney said, "Hurry, Tommy, the bell is about to ring." I left for the bathroom immediately. I had a plan. I was just going to walk right into the boy's bathroom and just start beating on him without saying one word. I couldn't believe I was doing this. I was so scared. I began to ask myself should I just punch him first, or should I throw him on the ground and start hitting him. But when I entered, Roman was in the first stall. This was a game-changer.

When I saw Roman's shoes pointing forward with his pants scrunched down around his ankles. I called an audible and completely changed my plans. I decided to quickly reach under the stall door, and steal his shoes. I thought it would be funny if he had to ride the bus home without his shoes. I figured he owed me a pair of shoes anyway. I quietly moved into position and hesitated for a moment. Then, just as I grabbed his shoes, the bell rang. I panicked and yanked my arms back, but I got more than just a pair of shoes.

I did get the shoes, but his shoes were accompanied by his socks, his pants and his underwear. Roman was in the stall wearing nothing but a T-shirt. He started yelling. I quickly turned away and just stuffed all of his clothes into my book bag as I ran out of the bathroom. I walked slowly down the hall to get on my bus and avoid suspicion. I got to my bus and sat there shaking with fear. I knew I had gone too far. I thought about policemen coming onto the bus to arrest me and put me in jail. I knew if my bus left the school. I was in the clear. It seemed like an eternity as I waited. I thought they were holding the buses and were looking for me. I hid my book bag under the seat and prayed my bus would leave soon. Finally, I heard the air brake release, and the bus started moving. I smiled as I stared back at the school, knowing Roman was still in the bathroom.

When I got home, I started to get scared again. I was so afraid of being caught I panicked. I got a plastic garbage bag and put Roman's socks, shoes, underwear and pants into it. I got on my bike and rode to the creek about a mile from our house. When I got there, I put some rocks in the bag and poked holes in it. I tied it up tight and threw it into the deepest part of the creek. The anxiety vanished as soon as the bag hit the water and sank to the bottom. As the bag gave up its last remaining bubbles, I smiled and casually rode back home. For the first time in quite a while, I was proud to be Tom Nardone.

The next day, I felt something on the bus I had never felt before. I felt anticipation. I could not wait to get to school and find out the sum of the damage I had done. I also brought something else I never had at school. I had confidence. I realized no longer did I have to allow people to bully me. I felt like a million bucks and wasn't afraid of anything or anybody. I knew it was going to be a great day, but it was far more than just a great day. It was many times better than I could have hoped. I wouldn't have believed anything I did could have produced such an amazing series of events. It was like a movie where everything falls beautifully into place.

The day began with Mrs. Lee, the principal, and Roman's parents standing in front of the whole class. Mrs. Lee began by explaining to us Roman ended up stranded in the bathroom until 6 p.m. the previous night. She went on to inform us a student stole all of his clothes while he was in the bathroom. There were no teachers working late because there were only a few more days of school until summer break began. Roman sat there on the toilet crying. Melvin, the janitor heard him and called his parents and explained the situation to them. They brought some clothes to the school for him, and it was just before 7 p.m. when he finally left.

His father was furious but said nothing. His mother was crying. Roman's mom pleaded with the class to tell them who was responsible, but no one knew a thing. She even talked about what a sweet boy her

31

Roman was and how he would never do anything to anyone. I wanted to jump up and tell her about what a great guy her son was, but I just held my tongue. I took delight in their pain, but I was wrong to feel this way. Roman's parents were not guilty as far as I knew.

As far as Roman's social standing went, my actions kicked it right in the nuts. Roman was in school the day following the class's interrogation, and I enjoyed the last three days of the first grade watching Roman take my place as the butt of all the jokes. I did not participate in the ridicule. It was enough for me to have been the cause of him sitting at his desk with his head down. He did not want the class to see he was crying.

I did feel bad later for his mom, and I still do. No mother wants to worry about her son's safety while he is away from her. At the time however, I was fine to see Roman's mom wearing the face of my own mother for a change. For whatever reason, this woman loved her little boy. I did what I did for nobody but myself. Today, I will say my actions were not wrong, and if given the choice, I would do it the exact same way. He deserved it, and if it still bothers him today, then I am sure it pales in comparison to what I felt. That was my first year of school.

I think Mrs. Sweeney was wrong. She should have been more worried about the way her students were behaving toward me than she was about whether or not we went to the bathroom without permission. I no longer resent Mrs. Sweeney, but I can't help but wonder if she had intervened would the rest of the class gotten to know me better. Would they have found me to be an interesting person? I suppose I will never know the answer.

My biggest problems in the first grade were social problems. I had lots of trouble paying attention and as the year went on I didn't even try to pay attention. I was too consumed by the way the class behaved toward me, and I just squeaked by academically. I didn't like my teacher, and I didn't like my classmates. I suppose you could say I learned a great deal in the first grade, but what I learned was not a part of the curriculum.

The second grade was better. I still had lots of trouble paying attention in class, but I had Mrs. Griffin as my teacher. I really liked her. Mrs. Griffin was aware of my challenges early on, and she took a special interest in me. She was very nice, and I know she cared about me. She was also a beautiful woman, and I had a bit of a crush on her. When we were learning states and their locations on the map. Mrs. Griffin had a big map of the United States on the wall up in the front of her room. She would stand up with her pointer and point to a state as the class would say its name aloud. I had no problem staring at her all day, so I learned where the states were in fairly short order.

I was not treated badly in her classroom by the other students. She was very active and did not stand by or sit at her desk very much. She walked around the room when she spoke, and this created an entirely new dynamic. There really was not much opportunity for the class to pick on me. She spent a great deal of time standing at or near my desk because somehow she knew I was prone to not pay attention. Though I daydreamed in her class often, she would always catch me. She would make a joke out of it, but not the kind of joke that would cause the class to give me a hard time. She never got mad about it. She is the reason I passed the second grade with little trouble.

Even though the whole class did not make fun of me in her classroom, I still took a lot of grief on the playground. I had to hear all the other students call me names, and they would rehash every silly thing I said in the classroom. I remember Mrs. Griffin laughing loudly at the things I said, but sometimes I went too far with my comments. She was quick to tell me the moment it happened. This was reason enough for the other students in my class to give me a hard time later on the playground. A few kids liked to pick on me every day as the others would watch, and sometimes it got out of hand. One of the kids would shove me and make threats. Every now and then, he would punch me in the arm or the chest. I just took it, and I guess I learned to deal with it since it was only thirty minutes out of the day.

One day on the playground, I met a very special person. His name was Brody Bricker. He was also in the second grade but in another class. They took recess at the same time as our class. I did not know him very well, but he quickly became my best friend. The day I saw him for the first time on the playground he was off playing by himself, and I thought this was a little strange. I went up and spoke to him, and he was very nice to me. I discovered he lived in the same neighborhood as me. We spoke, and he explained to me the other kids in his class did not like him very much either.

It wasn't long before some people in the classroom saw me talking to him, and they had to run over and tell Brody what kind of person they thought I was. I spoke up and told them to mind their own business. It was a young black girl who was giving me trouble, and when I spoke up she quickly said, "You shut yo mouth, you white cracka!" I will never forget the first time anyone stood up for me.

Brody Bricker looked at this girl and said. "You shut up! You graham cracker." She did not know what he meant, and they all just left us be. I managed to do what was necessary to pass, and I did go on to the third grade.

Third grade was tough as far as the schoolwork went. I had Mrs. Heatly. She was not as nice or pretty as Mrs. Griffin was, so I daydreamed all the time. She was not mean, but she had the difficult task of trying to teach me the multiplication tables. Every day I watched as the rest of the class went up to Mrs. Heatly's desk and would tell her they were ready for their quiz. At her desk, Mrs. Heatly would quietly ask them their three tables or their four tables. They would get them all correct, and they would get a gold star next to their name on the board. I was trailing behind the whole class. I had my ones tables and my tens tables completed, but nothing else.

The reason I had such a tough time with multiplication tables was I thought they were stupid. I did not understand why knowing the multiplication tables were so important. I had no interest in learning them, and I had things I wanted to do. I did not want to study for them, and for these reasons I was unable to learn them.

When I was studying them, I would become very frustrated. I would tell my mom how stupid I was because I couldn't figure it out. She hated hearing me say this knowing it wasn't true. I shouted this at the top of my lungs from my bedroom, so she would hear me and feel sorry for me. I wanted her to tell me I didn't have to learn them. My mother could not take it anymore and appealed to my father to intervene.

When I woke up for school Friday morning, my dad asked me if I wanted to go to work with him on Saturday. I loved being around my dad, and I could not have been more excited. I asked my dad questions all the time about what he did at work. When we got there, he asked me if I could help, and I agreed. My dad ran a printing press and made forms, envelopes and letterheads. When I asked him what he needed me to do, he stopped the press, walked over to a table and explained what he needed me to do. He asked me to figure things out for him that required the use of multiplication. When I could not do it, he showed me how. While he was showing me, he said he was glad to spend time with me, but it would have gone faster if I knew my multiplication tables. He told me if I could learn how to multiply, I would be able to be a better helper to him, and he would probably bring me with him to work more often.

This was all the motivation I needed. I asked my Dad a few questions throughout the day about specific multiplication problems, but by the time we left I stopped asking because I knew most of the answers. I went home that day excited because I realized the need for multiplication. I could use them to help my dad. It had been over a month since I began studying my multiplication tables, and I could not get past the ones and tens. In the span of a weekend, I learned them all the way through the nines. I was the first person in my class to see their name with twelve gold stars out to the side of it.

States and capitals were next, and I hated them. It was worse than the times tables. When I had trouble with them, I just went to dad and asked him why I needed to know the capitals for all the states. I thought since he knew why I needed to know the times tables he could surely explain the importance of this as well.

He thought for a moment, he smiled and said, "Come here, Tommy." I remember Dad whispering in my ear, "You don't really need to know what the capitals for all the states are, but if you could just do it for me, it would keep your mother and your teachers off my back. Okay?" When my father agreed with me, he sort of joined my team, and I was able to do this knowing it was helping him.

Looking back to these early days makes me physically ill. I was having problems not only with the other kids in social situations but also the work which was advancing in difficulty, and I developed an indifference to being at school. This was due largely to the way I was treated, but the work was starting to take a toll on me as well. When I was at school, all I thought about was how much longer it was going to be until it was time to leave. The only thing I liked about school was being on the playground with Brody Bricker.

In the beginning, I thought school was going to be a place to go and learn interesting things, meet new people and make friends. I thought it would be something I could do to make my parents proud of me. While I made only one friend, I did manage to make my parents proud of me up to this point. I had a lot of trouble with the schoolwork, but it was never anything major.

I saw only the things I thought were important and little else. What became important was being accepted and being liked. I decided I would settle for just not being made fun of, embarrassed or picked on.

This is what occupied my mind while I was in school. I spent time worrying about this more than anything else. My schoolwork took a backseat to trying to get past why people did not like me. I believe if I were not so preoccupied with fitting in, I would have learned more and perhaps made much better grades, rather than simply just passing by the skin of my teeth.

I was finding most of the people at school to be very impolite. I had strangely become so accustomed to being laughed at, I just kept quiet most of the time. I didn't get used to it. I was never okay with this treatment, but I just came to expect it every day. I felt as if the school was for the other kids, and I was not welcome there. I felt as if I was not supposed to be there. I was so consumed with not getting embarrassed in front of the class that I avoided speaking to people or asking the teacher questions.

I remember wondering what these other kids did to be treated so well by one another. I looked at them each day and wondered what it would be like to be them. What would it be like to have friends at school who were interested in me or in what I had to say? It shames me today to admit this, but it was true. At this young age, I would have rather been one of the other kids. I fantasized about this at school as I daydreamed.

Readiness, first, second and third grade were a challenge, but I managed to get through them with a few scrapes and bruises. Most of the problems at school stayed at school and had not ever followed me home.

Chapter 3

Brody Bricker was one of my best friends growing up. He stood up for me on the playground when no one else would. I lived a life of fear, and he had absolutely no fear. I spent more time with him than any of my other friends. I really liked Brody. I don't know why he liked me. I would never participate in his mischief except to be present and laugh at his antics.

He was definitely unique. I don't know if he was ADHD, but there was something off about him. I am amazed today that he never got me in any trouble. He lived to cause trouble. He would do anything to get a reaction out of someone or cause grief for an unknown person simply for his own amusement. He seemingly had no conscience and absolutely no fear. I often tried to talk him out of the things he planned to do. Sometimes I was successful, and sometimes I was not. I did not feel I was in a position to pick and choose my friends, but I don't regret being friends with Brody.

The Halloween when we were nine-years-old, I went to Brody's house before we went out trick-or-treating. When I arrived, he did not yet have his costume on. I went as Batman, and he was going to be Superman. When I entered the house, his mother told me to go back to his room.

When I entered his room, Brody said, "Hey, Tommy. Close the door." He then opened his window and threw a bag outside. I asked him what was in the bag and he said, "You'll see."

He put on his superman costume, and we left the house. As soon as the door shut, Brody ran to the side of his house to retrieve the bag he had thrown outside. He said, "Hey, c'mon, we have to go into the woods." When we got there Brody started emptying the bag. He pulled out a sheet, a can of red spray paint, and a long piece of string tied to a square piece of cardboard.

I asked him, "Brody man, what is all this stuff?"

He explained it was his real Halloween costume. He took off the superman stuff and put it in the bag. He asked for my assistance to help him wrap himself up tightly with the sheet from head to toe. We were able to configure it so he could still walk and use his hands. His next request was for me to spray-paint him with the can of red spray-paint he brought along. I did as he asked but I still had no idea what he was supposed to be. That was until he put on his little white shower cap and tied the string to it and I noticed the piece of cardboard hanging from the end of the string said, "Kotex®". He even put the little ® next to the logo.

I said, "Brody, no, man. You can't do this."

To which he replied, "It is already done let's go." Yes, on this Halloween, he decided to trick-or-treat as a used tampon.

I knew I should not be involved with him on this one, but my dad did say to stay with him while we were out and he did not want me walking the streets by myself on Halloween night. So, I just went under the banner of obeying my father.

The very first house we went to was incredible. It was the home of a single man. We knocked on the door, and he opened it and when we said, "trick or treat" this man stared at Brody and said nothing. He stared for about ten seconds and then began laughing harder than I could believe. He could barely hold the bowl of candy. He was laughing and it went on and on. As he laughed, he just looked at Brody and said, "You win!!!" With that he dumped half the bowl in my bag and the other half in Brody's and then closed the door and shut off all the outside lights on his house. I am sure we made his Halloween.

We thought this was amazing, and we could not wait to get to the next house. I really thought Brody was on to something. We did not get the same warm reception at the next house. A lady answered the door dressed as Mary Poppins and her small children were with her dressed as little angels. She took one look at Brody, and she lost it. She ordered her two little girls away and told him how awful he was and literally chased us out of her yard.

As you might expect all of the men laughed and all of the women went psycho. We were getting way more candy because the men could not contain their laughter, and they all felt the need to reward Brody for his imagination. I was equally rewarded by proxy.

We were having a blast, but some woman must have called the police. We saw the blue lights coming down the road entering the street we were on and Brody said, "Hey, I wonder who they are after." They stopped right in front of us, and Brody started running. The cop told me to stay put, but he could not catch Brody because he was laughing so hard.

The police officer came back and told me to get in the car. I started crying because I thought I was being arrested. He let me sit in the front seat to convince me I was not in trouble. He wanted me to help him find Brody and to tell him how to contact his parents if need be. I remember the dispatcher mentioning all units to be on the lookout for a runaway tampon, and she was laughing on the radio.

We drove a little more and the police officer saw Brody running through someone's front yard and he hit the siren. This scared Brody, and he tripped. The cop got out and spoke to him a moment and put him in the back of the car. I had to tell him how to get back to Brody's house. The cop was laughing so hard when we got there, he just got out of the car, and I watched through the windshield as he escorted this tampon to the front door. The cop was laughing so hard he could not say a word. He just handed Brody over to his dad and walked back to the car.

I convinced him not to tell my dad what Brody had done, and he just dropped me off a little way from my house. As I walked home, from the drop site, I was imagining what my father would have done if I had done such a thing. It scared me to think of what my father's reaction. I imagined how embarrassed he would have been having the neighbors know his son as the boy who went as a tampon for Halloween. This was the difference between Brody and me. He didn't think about any of that.

Brody was grounded for three weeks after that. His dad made him go to every house and apologize to them, for his portrayal of a used tampon. In addition, he was not allowed to trick-or-treat ever again without an adult chaperon.

It was normal for me to spend the night at Brody's house on the weekends. One weekend, Brody had gotten a new tent for his birthday. He wanted to have me over so we could camp in the backyard. I was sure he must have some other reason for wanting to be outside in a tent, but I had never been camping so I thought it would be fun. I went over to his house, and we set it up. It got dark, and we entered the tent.

We were out there for a while, but we got bored, and Brody asked me if I felt like going swimming. Since Brody did not have a pool, I asked "Where are we supposed to go swimming?"

He said "My next door neighbors are out of town." I was too scared, so I told him no. He hounded me for 20 minutes, but I was not going to risk it. Brody was mad, but he said he would go by himself.

He walked into the yard, stripped down completely naked, and climbed the fence. I could not believe he was willing to take such a risk. He entered the pool at the shallow end and quietly swam from one side of the pool to the other. During his sixth lap or so, while he was in the deep end, the lights in and around the pool came on. He quickly went for the ladder, but it was too late.

The backdoor opened slowly, and the lady of the house came out for a late night swim. Brody was hiding by the ladder, with his head low, trying to avoid detection. She came out with her towel and laid it over a chair. Brody was calm and did not panic. He actually had a plan to escape. The lady went to the diving board, and prepared for her entry into the pool. She dove. The second she entered the water Brody darted up the ladder and exited the pool, but he wasn't fast enough.

When she surfaced after her dive, she saw Brody's naked ass leaving her pool and began to scream so loud that it scared me. Brody kept going. He ran into the woods at top speed and did so while naked. This lady did not stop screaming even as she ran into the house forgetting her towel.

Less than five minutes later the cops showed up. There were three cars with their lights on. One of them went to the house, and the other two were patrolling the neighborhood looking for a naked boy. Brody was gone for two hours. I had no idea where he was or when he was coming back. I thought about going to look for him, but I did not want to end up taking the fall for him, so I lay back down in the tent pretended to be asleep.

Brody returned after being in the woods for three hours. The pool washed off all of his mosquito repellent, and they feasted on his naked ass for three hours. He had scrapes all over his body. When he got to the tent he asked me very nicely, "Tom, will you please go over to the fence and get my clothes?" I thought that the risk of walking to the fence and back was a better prospect than having to sleep next to a naked boy. I went and got them without incident.

Shortly after Brody got dressed, he was laughing about the whole thing. He was so proud of himself for evading the police department, and he hoped the story would be on the news. He told me about places he hid and for how long. The only thing I could think about while he was gone was whether or not he was going to get caught and if I was going to be involved in it with him. I was paranoid the whole night.

Brody's parents did not trust him. They knew me be a good kid, and they trusted me. One summer, Brody called me very excited. His mom had decided to take him to Jekyll Island for a summer vacation. He was thrilled when his mom said that he could invite me to go with them. His mom thought a lot of me, and she told my parents she would pay for everything. My parents were fine with it and told me not to let him get me into any trouble. They knew Brody was a bad kid, but they knew no specific details of things he had done.

I was eleven years old and had never been to the ocean. We left early one morning and got there around lunchtime. After we checked into our hotel room, Brody's mom said she was going to the pool and we could do "whatever".

We decided to go to the beach. It was so much fun swimming against the waves and letting them wash me up on the shore. Brody was having a good time, too. For a moment, I thought maybe Brody would not resort to his normal shenanigans this trip. I was wrong.

After swimming for about two hours, Brody said, "Hey Tom, I have to use the bathroom. Come with me. I don't know if I will remember where the hotel room is." I agreed so we grabbed our towels and went toward the parking lot.

This was a very big hotel complex. The walk back to the room was a good ten minutes, and we had to walk across the parking lot which was a giant plane of black asphalt. I explained to Brody that it would take a while, and he said, "Well, I am not walking that far." I knew by the way he said this there was going to be trouble.

Shortly after we began our journey across the parking lot, Brody started searching for car doors which were unlocked. I said, "Brody, are you crazy? What are you doing?"

He said "Don't worry about it, Tommy, and lower your voice. I don't wanna get caught." He checked a lot of cars, and I was getting irritated and paranoid. Just as I was about to say something else, he found an unlocked car. It was a beautiful silver Cadillac. I really did not know what his plans were, but I was scared to death.

Brody said, "Tom, go stand over there. You are not going to want to watch what comes next." I, of course, obliged him and walked far enough away to not see any details, but close enough to see what he was doing. Brody took his swim trunks off and entered the back seat of this Cadillac while completely naked in broad daylight. He put his feet on the lip of the back seat, and his ass in front of the backseat head rest.

41

He put his hands on the head rests of the front seats. What happened next was one of the worst things I had ever seen.

Brody was obviously having some kind of gastric issues. When the bomb bay doors opened, he dropped the entire payload. It was awful. I could hear the awful sounds from fifty feet away. At first he was laughing so hard he couldn't talk, but then the smell hit him, and I saw him start to gag. It got to be too much, and he started to throw up. He was having a tough time in there as you might imagine. The smell was bad enough, but with the heat it must have been unbearable. Then finally, he seemed to be finished. I was so relieved. I just knew he would get out of the car, close the door, get dressed, and then we could leave, but not just yet.

I was worried we were going to get caught at this point. I asked, "Brody, what are you doing now?"

He immediately resumed his laughter and said "I am almost done. I have to wipe." He got out of the back seat and closed the door, still with no pants on, and laughing. He opened the front door, and entered the car for the second time. I had to go in for a closer look. I watched him place the crack of his ass on the lip of the front seat. He then carefully pulled himself from one side of this Cadillac to the other, dragging his ass across it, using the entire length of the front seat to de-soil himself. It reminded me of a dog dragging it's ass across the yard or the carpet.

Finally, Brody closed up the car and locked it. He put his trunks on looked at me as if nothing had happened and said, "You want to go swim some more?"

For the rest of the day, I could not stop thinking about the hot Georgia sun baking the unholy mess that Brody left in that Cadillac. I wondered what kind of reaction these people were going to have when they found that their car, for no reason other than it had been made into a crime scene.

Thinking back, I just hope that whoever owned that car was some sex offender or rapist or any other person that the world deems as undesirable. As an eleven year old kid, it was just funny.

Brody's appetite for trouble was not reserved only for complete strangers. He was perfectly okay causing harm to anyone who crossed him or inconvenienced him. Even his own family would suffer at the expense of his entertainment. No one more than his father. I could not believe the difference in the way he felt towards his father compared to the way I felt towards mine.

Brody's father decided it was time for a new car, and he took Brody with him to the dealership. His dad decided on a model that resembled the 80s Plymouth Horizon. It came in many colors, and Brody liked the blue one. He told his dad the blue one looked the best, and it was the car he should buy. His dad however, decided on this ugly dark brown car that had some orange eagle painted on both doors and on the hood. This made Brody furious.

He called me when they got back and told me how stupid his father was and how embarrassed he would be to even have this car in the driveway. Brody and I had planned for me to spend that weekend at his house, as I did on many weekends in the summer.

When I got to Brody's house, the subject of the car came up immediately when his dad saw me and wanted to show it to me. He even told me and Brody to get in so I could take a ride in it. He was very proud of this car.

Later that night after his parents went to bed, Brody and I got up and sneaked out to do God knows what. When we got back he said "Hold on, Tom, I have to take a leak." He then proceeded to walk up to his Dad's new car, open the gas cap door, unscrew the cap, and pee into the tank. I could not believe what I was seeing. Brody saw the look of amazement on my face and began to laugh. He said, "Stop making me laugh, it is affecting my aim." He finished, zipped up, and we went back into his house and went to bed.

The next morning Brody and I woke up, and his dad was washing the car. He asked if we wanted to help him wax it. Brody knew I would say yes, so he quickly interrupted and said we are going over to Johnny and Billy's house and would be back later. So we left. We did not go to Johnny and Billy's house, but Brody and I stayed gone long enough to make sure his dad's car was done being waxed.

As we got back, Brody noticed his dad's car had all the doors open including the hatchback. He looked at me and said, "Come on." Brody went up to his dad's car, walked around to the rear of it, and began to pee into the open hatchback onto the carpet.

I said, "Brody, he is going to smell that for sure dude. How are you going to explain this?" He assured me he had it under control, and damned if he didn't.

Brody closed all the doors and windows of the car. We went inside, and Brody went right up to his dad and said "Dad, we closed your doors to your car."

He asked, "Why did you do that? I was airing it out to get rid of that new car smell."

Brody told him, "Well, there was some strange cat that was asleep in it, so we got rid of him and closed the doors so he would not come back."

His dad replied, "Oh! Thanks, Brody."

Brody said, "Sure, it was nothing."

That weekend I don't think he pissed anywhere but in that car. He did it several times in the gas tank, and several times in the cabin. It didn't matter what he did for that whole weekend. His dad would assume that the cat pissed in it.

The next morning Brody told me that he would have to cut the grass that day before we did anything. I said fine, and Brody said he had to set the stage. He went outside and gathered up a bunch of gravel and broken bricks and strategically placed them in the tall grass.

He came back inside and said "Tom, come outside and watch me cut the grass." I didn't care, so I went. He kept laughing while he was cutting the grass. I did not know why then. I figured it out before it happened, and I was too afraid to do anything about it. Brody had placed the bricks and gravel so that when he ran over it with the lawn mower, the shoot of the mower would be aimed at his dad's car. The purpose of the gravel was to act as shrapnel.

Brody came around, and he was so excited that he could not stand it. I knew he was about to run those bricks over, and I had my back turned, not wanting to see this, but I could not resist the show. When I turned, I saw his dad. I thought his dad was still inside. I looked at Brody, pointed at his dad whose back was turned and shook my head saying "No!" Brody, with a smile, nodded his head saying "Yes!"

Seconds later Brody, with his Dad's brand new lawnmower, hit the pile of gravel, and the test was a remarkable success. Brody's dad had turned into the line of fire just as it began. Brody sprayed a hail storm of gravel at his father and the car. It lasted longer than I thought it would have. There were scratches and dings all over the car. Brody's dad was going insane. He was jumping up and down telling Brody to turn off the mower. Brody was laughing so hard and with the lawnmower going he could not hear his Dad.

I don't know who took more fire, the car or his father. When the shooting was over, Brody just kept going like he didn't even notice that it had happened. His dad went running after him and started kicking his ass. Brody fought back, and they exchanged blows in the front yard on this blissful Sunday morning. Brody's mom came out, and Brody started his fake crying. When his mother saw that she started kicking Brody's dad's ass. Eventually the excitement stopped. Brody and I went to go play on the direction of his mother.

Later that day, Brody and I went back to his house. He was full of anticipation at the thought of looking at this car. He wanted to see the damage he had done. When we got to the car, he was disappointed. I asked him what the matter was. He said "Well, my dad had to be out here screwing with the car. I was hoping to break a window. His fat-ass took most of the heavy gravel. Shit, let's go inside."

Over the next few months his dad was back and forth with the dealership trying to figure out why the car ran so poorly or sometimes not at all. It when finally got fixed Brody stopped peeing in the gas tank. He just sort of got bored with it all.

I was often in fear of what Brody would do next. He did not often heed my warnings. This is why he would not tell me when he was planning on doing things. I liked Brody and was drawn to the excitement. It was something I did not see much of in my life. I could not bear the thought of not knowing what he would do next.

One Saturday Brody and I decided to go to the movies. We were taking a shortcut through the woods to go to the movie theater. We had done this many times before, but this time we ran into some kids who were playing in the tree house in a yard we had cut through without incident in the past. We tried to just ignore them, but they had some problem with us cutting through their yard and told us to go around. We said we were sorry, and we started to go around, but that suddenly was not good enough either.

They wanted to fight. One of the kids said, "Now, we are gonna kick your asses."

Brody said, "Great, which one of you assholes wants to go first."

I did not want to fight, but if they were going to insist, then fine. Two of them came forward, one at me and one at Brody. The rest of them scurried up the tree house ladder to get a better view. We were doing great, and the kids we were fighting ran away. Then the kids in the tree house started yelling and throwing things at us. We got out of there just in case their parents decided to come out and raise hell about the two of us beating the hell out of their idiot sons.

Brody enjoyed beating those kids up, but he was angry that we ended up missing the movie we planned to go see. We were both scuffed up and were not able to get to the movie on time as our shortcut was not available. We decided to go back to his house. Brody was unhappy about this, and he did not speak the way back.

I was spending the night with him that night, and as usual, we sneaked out after it was dark outside. Brody said to me "Tom, wait here for just a minute." He came back with a duffel bag and said, "Okay, let's go." I didn't know where we were going, and he wouldn't tell me because he did not want me to chicken out, which I definitely would have.

As we were walking through the woods, I said, "Brody, we are going through the woods. Why didn't you just tell me we're going to the movies?"

He said, "We aren't going to the movies tonight." When he said that, I figured out what we were doing. I knew we were going back to the tree house where those kids were playing. When we got there, Brody told me to stay where I was, he would only be a minute. He climbed the chain link fence that surrounded the yard where the tree house stood. He quietly sneaked through the yard and went up the ladder and into the tree house.

This was not some half-ass tree house. The person who built this took time and money to make it very beautiful. It had a shingled roof and siding. Brody later told me that it even had a refrigerator and lights in it.

Brody was in the tree house for at least five very long minutes. He emptied the refrigerator into the duffel bag, along with any other snacks, or things of value. Finally I saw him coming out of the tree house and down the ladder. I gave a sigh of relief, but this night had only just begun.

I noticed Brody was messing with some rope on the way down the ladder. He then pulled out a lighter and lit the string. The string started burning very fast, I remember watching the flame as it was traveling up toward the tree house. All of a sudden WAHHHHH!! Out of the windows came a giant cloud of orange flames. Brody wasn't counting on the flames to be so bright. I had no idea what the hell he was doing until I saw this. I completely freaked out, and ran back towards his house which was a good mile through the woods. He jumped the fence and said "Tom, we better haul some ass." I was so far ahead that I barely heard him.

We were running through the woods, and within two minutes we could hear the fire engine horns and sirens. I turned back and saw flashing blue and red lights through the woods. I didn't care to sightsee for long. We got back to house and went right to bed. Brody wanted to talk about it because he was so proud of the mayhem he had caused. I was too scared. I felt like a criminal. Brody was laughing all night long as he imagined those kids waking up to see their house was burning.

I went home the next morning because it was too scary to be at Brody's anymore for the weekend. My dad was watching cartoons when I got home. As I walked in the door, my dad said, "Hey, you're home early. You want to watch Tom & Jerry?"

That sounded safe enough, so I said "Sure." I always enjoyed watching cartoons with my dad.

We were watching television for a while. I actually started to forget about what had happened the night before. I had gotten past it, and then the morning news came on. It was the tree house. The news was there covering an arson investigation. Apparently, the entire tree house burned up, along with the tree, and a shed. They showed the kids whose tree house it was, and they were crying. My dad said, "Boy, Tommy, what kind of sick sons of bitches would burn down a little kid's tree house?"

I said, "Only the meanest kind of person, Dad."

Moments later the phone rang. I knew it was Brody. I jumped up and got the phone and said, "Hello." He saw the news like I did, and he wanted to brag and tell me how awesome it was that his work was being covered by the news media. He asked, "Are you watching the news?"

I said, "Yes."

"Did you see those assholes crying? And we even got their dick dad's shed as a bonus."

I said, "Okay, I will be over later today," and hung up.

Dad asked, "Was that your friend, Brody?"

"Yes."

He said, "That sounds like some shit he would do."

I simply and truthfully replied, "I was with him all right, Dad."

I have never been more terrified than I was this night. I did keep hanging out with him because there was never a dull moment. He was fearless, and I always wanted to know what was next. My parents knew of the trouble I was having in school, so they allowed me to continue to be friends with Brody. They were not aware of the depth of his evil or they never would have let me near him.

Today, I believe that Brody was my friend, and he accepted me. He was lazy just like I was. We did have a lot in common. I think I enjoyed living vicariously through his actions. I am not proud to have been involved in all the things he did. I am even to this day ashamed of some of it. I did not have any other friends from school, and Brody and I always had fun together.

Watching him was exciting, fun and I was not sure what he would do next. Hanging out with him was far more interesting than me doing what I was supposed to be doing. He was living a dream I had to be free of the constraints I let people put on me. Seeing him do the things he did was fun. I wondered what it felt like to move about the earth with no fear. I lived this way vicariously through Brody.

While Brody was my friend, he was also a distraction from all of the trouble I made for myself as a result of my ADHD. I knew the risk of being friends with Brody Bricker, but he was interesting. He was different and did not think or act like anyone I had ever met. I wondered why he liked me and why I seemed to be his only friend. I suppose he had just as hard a time making friends as I did or maybe I was the only kid who did not have enough sense to realize the dangers of a friendship with him.

Chapter 4

Fourth grade was without a doubt the worst year I spent in elementary school. My fourth grade teacher's name was Mrs. Hayter. She was very nice to me, and I liked her, at least in the beginning. Prior to fourth grade, I was having trouble paying attention. My parents, T-ball coach and teachers all had repeatedly told me, "Tommy! You need to pay attention!" I heard this from so many people in my life, it just became trite and lost its meaning. In spite of my lack of paying attention, my grades had for the most part been passing.

My life was about to change because my days at school would no longer end at the final bell. In the fourth grade, I was introduced to homework. Homework brought everything bad in my life to a boil. Until the fourth grade, I only thought about school while I was at school. I never had any homework. Aside from studying times tables and the states and capitals, I never even thought about school while I was at home, and my life at home was separate.

Mrs. Hayter gave us class assignments and homework assignments. There were many ways in which I failed at completing and turning in my homework. I forgot to bring home the book I needed, so even though I listened and wrote down the assignment, I was unable to do my homework. I occasionally forgot to write down the assignment, and of course have no idea what I was supposed to do with the book on the occasions I did manage to bring it home with me.

I wrote down the assignment and brought the book home, but I was unable to read my own writing and, therefore, was unable to complete the assignment. I brought home the wrong book or forgot where I wrote the assignment and mistakenly used the paper I wrote it on to make a paper airplane on the school bus. There were times in math class Mrs. Hayter instructed us to do the even problems that night, but I didn't listen, so I flipped a coin and did the odd problems. It was always something. It was amazing how few times I actually turned in a homework assignment without any complications.

Every now and then, I got it right. I guess I did it correctly about half the time, but then there was the part where I had to turn in my work. This was every bit as big a problem as doing the work itself. Even though I spent hours at home working on my assignment, I went to school the next day without it. If I did manage to bring my homework to school, it was still no guarantee of a success.

In the mornings, Mrs. Hayter asked us to turn in our homework, but I was unable to find my work in the chaotic mess that was my book bag. I knew my assignment was in there somewhere. I was sure of it. I found lots of things in there when I looked for my assignments, but rarely found them. I had all sorts of things in it from other classes, my lunch or just something I found on the ground I wanted to keep. When this happened, I decided it was time to clean out my book bag.

My mother helped me with my homework when I needed her to. She became furious about halfway through my assignments when she realized we were doing an assignment we had already completed before. She ordered my bag brought to her and be dumped on the floor in the den. After a brief search, we found the assignment. I completed assignments with my mother, only to find out the next day when I turned them in for partial credit, I had already turned this assignment in on time.

I normally did not pay attention when Mrs. Hayter gave the class instructions. Instead of listening to my teacher, I was thinking about a show I watched on TV the previous night, or maybe looking out the window or playing with my lunchbox. I did not hear a word she said. I often had no clue we even had homework. Countless times she asked for the class to turn in our homework, and I had this, "Oh my God, what homework?" look on my face. I rationalized the fact I did not know we had homework. I told myself even if I did hear the assignment, there was a good chance I would not have it to turn in anyway.

It wasn't just the homework with which I struggled. My daydreaming was out of control. I was inside my own head, thinking about everything other than what I should have been. It was after these daydreams, I noticed the rest of the class was working quietly, and I had no idea what I was supposed to be doing. I had no one I could ask. I realized this would be another zero, and I could do nothing about it. So, I just shrugged it off and went back to my daydream until it was time to go home for the day.

All of this made me hate the fourth grade. Everything I did was wrong in some way. I only turned in half the work, and the half I did turn in I did very poorly, unless it was one my mother oversaw. I was so miserable I did not want to do anything on the weekends. I wanted to just sit around the house all day and do nothing in an attempt to make the weekends drag on endlessly.

Monday always came and with it, another week of new and innovative ways I could fail at what was asked of me. For a while, I went in every Monday morning with an attitude, as if to say, "I am going to listen and make sure I turn everything in on time." After failing at this, week after week, I finally just gave up and quit trying all together. The closer it came to report card day, the less I tried. I figured my grades were so bad, a good week would not have made enough of a difference to affect my report card anyway.

I was so depressed every day in school. I was usually defeated before the day began. Mrs. Hayter asked me one Friday afternoon, "Tommy, are you excited it's Friday?"

"No, ma'am," I said, and she looked at me with surprise.

"Well, the weekend is almost here," she responded.

"Yes, ma'am, but in two days, it will just be Monday again." She looked at me with concern and gently shook her head.

As it happens, my wanting to sit around the house all the time and do nothing turned out to be very convenient desire. Following the report card I received, it made my ending up on restriction a rather smooth transition. During the second and third grade, I periodically went up and asked the teacher what my current grade was, but in fourth grade, I did not want to know. I just wanted to sit and hope somehow my grades were not as bad as I imagined they were. I hoped somehow I would just get lucky and receive good grades in spite of all I had not done. Sadly, I was not that lucky. When report cards came out, I prepared for the worst. When Mrs. Hayter came around, I took mine and slowly opened it. I was not very happy to see my grades. When I looked at my report card, I said to myself, "Well, at least I got two Ds."

I spent the whole day trying to come up with answers to the questions my parents were sure to have as to why this happened. I thought for a while, and I determined there were no answers. There was only the truth. I was holding this truth in my hands. When I got home, I did not even turn on the TV while I waited for my father to come home. I sat down on the sofa in our den for two hours in silence. This silence was not to be confused with the type of silence people find relaxing. This silence was the calm before the storm. The silence was broken as I heard the worst sound I had heard all day long. This sound ushered in the beginning of the most colossal shit-storm I would ever see.

The sound was the engine of my dad's truck pulling into the driveway. I listened as it got louder and closer, and then it went silent. I heard the slam of his door. After a short delay, I heard the sound of his footsteps walking up the wooden steps and across the back porch. I remember the sunlight against the blinds, interrupted by his shadow as he walked past the window. I heard the jingling of his keys as he unlocked the door. The door opened, and it was Dad with a big smile on his face. He was in a fantastic mood. He looked at me and said in a cheerful tone of voice, "Hey, Tommy! How was school today, bud?" At that moment, Dad was actually glad to see me. It was now time for me to remove the smile from his face as only I could.

As I watched him gaze upon my report card for the first time, I could almost feel the clouds of brown rolling in above my house, and so began the dreaded storm. This exchange between my father and me was as amazing as I predicted. I handed my report card to him, and watched as this happy, smiling man morph into an insane person. It was as if my father left his own body and was replaced by a raging lunatic. My dad could go from zero to warp speed without even shifting gears. He looked at me and began as he always did, "Aw, you gotta be shittin' me!" This was his favorite tag line. He was a wordsmith like no one I have ever known. He began shouting at the top of his lungs, and he never found himself at a loss for words. He didn't even need to pause to think or gather his thoughts. He seemed to pull every word out of a holster, and he fired them at me with a deadly accuracy. I was always so envious of his ability to do that.

When this show began, I cried as my dad started yelling, but fifteen minutes into his presentation, he was in reruns. I eventually stopped crying and was then able to listen more attentively for a while. I think he was about two hours into it when my mother came home. I could see the relief on my father's face as my mom walked in and said, "What is all the yelling about?" Dad handed her my report card, waited for my mom to start yelling and then went into the kitchen to fix himself a sandwich and an iced tea. He was yelling so long he became exhausted and needed to recharge.

During my mother's session, my father interrupted me every time I gave my mother an answer he didn't like. He did this with his mouth full. I couldn't understand anything he said except the swear words. So, I got most of it. I always listened to my dad when he yelled at me, but after two hours I was getting bored. During my mother's words I mentally checked out, and both my parents noticed. My mother said, "Dammit, Tommy, are you listening to me?"

I was about to lie and say I was, but my dad, with a mouth full of sandwich yelled, "Shit no, he isn't listening to you, Susan. Look at him. He is counting the bricks on the fireplace!" My mother asked me if I thought she was talking to hear herself talk. I said no. By this time, Dad had finished eating and come out of the kitchen. My parents tagged, and now my dad was back on the job.

I don't really know how long this went on, but it was about 4:30 p.m. when it began, and I know it was way past dark when Mom decided to shut it down. I remember it was past my bedtime, but apparently this was very important, so my dad authorized a later bedtime. I was allowed to eat in silence afterward, and then I just went on to bed for the night. I couldn't possibly remember everything he said, but I can hit some of the highlights. I got so many of these from dad they just seem to run together.

"Tommy, what in the hell is this? I'll tell you what this is. This is SHIT for grades! I don't know whether I should sign this report card or wipe my ass with it."

"What the hell have you been doing for six weeks? I wouldn't think it were possible for your thumb to be up your ass that long. Was your thumb cold?"

"Tommy, I know you are a smart kid, but you just don't give a SHIT!"

"Are you insane?"

"Do you know what would happen if I went to work and did what you do in school? They would fire my ass just like that, and we would live in the street."

Dad asked a question. I answered him "Dad, I thought...." He would interrupt me and say, "You thought? What the hell did you use?"

"Tommy I don't know what there is more of, lead in your ass or shit in your brains?"

"Tommy, I sure am glad my life doesn't depend on your speed."

As I stated earlier, he was a wordsmith.

My dad was also not a huge fan of the answer "I don't know." Dad was less than pleased with my progress or in my lack thereof. Dad believed I was being lazy and just didn't care. Even though the thunder of his voice rolled on for what seemed an eternity, one thing he kept repeating was, "Tommy, I know you are a smart kid, but you just don't give a shit!" From his point of view, it looked just that way. Mom during her time did not yell, and her words did not quite have the same color as my father's did. She just kept saying, "Tommy, you are just as lazy as the day is long."

What my parents saw was their son who was lying around all day watching TV. Then, I bring home a piece of paper containing what my

53

dad referred to as "shit for grades". I couldn't blame them for being angry. Restriction was not a big deal to me, but I now had no choice but to stay indoors for a little while. The last thing my dad said to me I would never forget. He always finished the report card ass-chewing show by saying, at the top of his lungs, "Now, go into your room and box up everything that brings you happiness and bring it to me! You can have it back when you learn to give a shit! Bring me another report card like this, and I'll destroy it all by running over it with my truck!"

I always went to my room and cried after Dad yelled at me. It wasn't because he grounded me and I couldn't go outside, and it wasn't because I thought he did not love me; I never doubted his love for me. I was upset because I let down the greatest man I knew. I cried any time I ever let my father down. It was the hardest part. I was not living up to his expectations. My father was disappointed in me. I could not bear the man who was my hero to be disappointed in me.

Twenty or thirty minutes after it ended, my dad did as he always did after yelling at me. He came into my room and sat with me and told me he loved me. He made me understand why he was angry, and he told me not to worry. We would get past all of this.

I have to say he was right about most of what he said to me while he was yelling. I didn't care. Sure, I cared while he was shouting at me. I cared when I was crying and when I could see how disappointed in me he was, but this was only one night of my life. It was one night of Dad screaming, and then it was all over. I knew I would be back at school the next day making the same mistakes in spite of my efforts. The only future I could see for myself was six of weeks of ridicule by my fellow students, six weeks of forgotten homework, six weeks of zeroes because I could not pay attention and six weeks of restriction.

If this was not enough, now there would be something new to be added to my day. I would have six weeks of daily interrogations about my day. When my parents got home, I would sit down with my mom and/or my dad and dissect every single moment of my horrific day in an attempt to help them to help me. This was a nightly disaster. I could not recall the things from my day and would always respond with my father's least favorite words: I don't know.

It was as if my father's words had no impact on me because I just did not care anymore. I was angry at my parents because they did not seem to understand how I felt when I was at school. It wasn't just the way I was treated. It was the entire disappointment machine. It was my classmates, my schoolwork, my fear of punishment from my parents, and all of the daily personal failures I experienced. None of it was ever absent from my thoughts. I respected my parents, and I loved them both. I knew they wanted me to do better in school, but when you try as hard as you can and continue to disappoint the ones you love, you begin to lose faith in yourself. This is what happened to me. It was for this reason I quit caring.

There was one positive thing I had left at school, and that was Mrs. Hayter. In spite of my grades, Mrs. Hayter was very nice to me and never really gave me a hard time. I could always go to her, and even if the answer was not what I wanted to hear. She always showed empathy and compassion, but then the unthinkable happened.

A couple of weeks after I got my report card, Mrs. Hayter gave the class an opportunity to get an extra 15 minutes of recess on Friday. It was Thursday, and she made a deal with the class. She said if everyone stayed in their seat and did not talk, for the last 15 minutes of class we could have extra recess on Friday. Well, guess who was not listening to her as she made this offer. I was busy trying to catch up on homework. I did not hear one word she said.

The rest of the class was quietly sitting. I was almost done with my homework, but my pencil broke, and I needed to sharpen it. Having no clue about any contract she had presented to the class, I got up and went to the pencil sharpener as I always did when my pencil broke. I will never forget the whole class staring at me as I walked across the room. Mrs. Hayter did not see me because her back was turned, but as soon as she heard the pencil sharpener she turned around and let me have it.

"Tommy Nardone! What is your problem? Did you forget to bring your thinking cap this morning?" The class roared with laughter, and Mrs. Hayter went on to say, "You know you can get one real cheap at the store!" Then the rest of the class began to tell me where I could go to buy a thinking cap. Mrs. Hayter even thanked one little girl who recommended another place I could buy one. The laughter continued but was quickly stifled by the final bell. Everybody got up and left to go to their buses. I was so angry, but I said nothing. The bell had rang, and I could not get to my bus fast enough. The class was relentless in their remarks as we went out to our buses. This hurt me past the point of tears. I was furious, and I knew I would tell my mother of this. I couldn't take anymore.

When my mom and dad asked me during my nightly post-school interrogation how my day went, I started crying. I had to tell them. My mom hit the roof when I told her. She had an idea people were picking on me but hearing about the teacher leading the charge was more than she was going to indulge. She rarely got involved with my teachers since she was a teacher herself. This ended up as a parent/teacher conference the next day. My mother was not about to let one of my teachers join the students as they mocked me. My father was also at this meeting.

I will never forget how upset Mrs. Hayter was to hear how her words hurt me so badly. She was crying uncontrollably, and I knew she was sincere in her apology, but I could never trust her again. I did not have the ability to look at her as anything but the enemy. For the rest of the year, in spite of her kindness, I always viewed her just as I saw the rest of the class. She was, and would forever be, one of them.

When report cards came out, I saw I had only done marginally better than before. I looked at it and noted all the failing grades and just rolled my eyes and put it in my book bag. I just didn't care anymore. When I got home, I put my report card in the middle of the table where the interrogations took place. I went into my room, turned out the lights and went to bed. I slept for hours. When I woke up later that evening, I was surprised no one woke me. I was sure my dad would want to talk about my report card for a few hours.

I was thirsty, so I went into the kitchen to get some water, and my dad was there. Dad saw me and calmly said, "Hey, Tommy."

I said, "Hey, Dad." I got my drink and started to walk back to my room.

Dad said, "Tommy, come here, son. I want to talk to you." He wasn't mad. He was speaking to me in his most calm, normal voice. He did not yell, and he exhibited no anger. We just talked. I don't remember everything he said, but he took me off restriction and told me just to do the best I could.

I said, "Okay." I was taken off restriction, and somehow I managed to improve more each reporting period.

It was near the end of the year, and it looked as though I was going to pass. I was pleased, and so were my parents. My grades did get better. Things at home were for the most part back to normal, but my classmates in Mrs. Hayter's class would never let up. They were every bit as mean to me as the kids in the first grade. I was content to just ride out the rest of the year without any drama and hope for a better fifth grade year.

I had forgiven Mrs. Hayter for her insensitive words, but not the rest of the class. Their mockery was ongoing. It was about three weeks until the last day of school, and we were just killing time until it was over. One of the ways we killed time was to prepare for the upcoming Field Day event. This is where the entire class competed in athletic events with the other fourth grade classes. The winning class would get an ice cream party. I decided this is where I would deliver the ultimate "Screw you!" to all of the assholes who made my life a living hell all year.

While we were practicing for Field Day, it was determined I could throw the Frisbee farther than anyone else in my class. Mrs. Hayter quickly signed me up for this event. I had every intention of taking first place at this event and getting the coveted blue ribbon. Some of my classmates were actually happy to see me throw it so far and even congratulated me. This meant nothing to me, but one of the kids came up to me and said something along the lines of "Wow, you did something right. Try not to lose this for the whole class."

This comment was a game-changer, and the one I appreciated most. I took his comment as an opportunity to balance the scales a little bit. I decided on Field Day I would use this as a chance to stick it in and break it off inside the entire class. There would be no ice cream party my class's future. I would see to it. I would do everything I could to prevent them for receiving any type of reward. I sure as hell was not going to aid in their efforts. Those kids might not remember much of their fourth grade year. Maybe some of them would not remember anything about it, but I was sure none of them would ever forget the name Tommy Nardone.

After our week of practice, I was in three events: the wheel barrel race, the Frisbee throw and the tug-o-war. I was placed in the wheel barrel race by default, which is to say they did not have enough people. I was obviously in that Frisbee throw because I was just awesome, but the whole class was in the tug-o-war. I could not wait to get into my events. I was excited about Field Day, so much so I could not sleep the night before. I felt as I often felt on Christmas Eve. I was going to wipe the smiles off all of their faces.

I was surprised on Field Day to see so many of the parents showed up. This pleased me greatly. I couldn't wait to see their faces either. They were all guilty by association as far as I was concerned. One thing they all had in common was they all had assholes for kids. My parents were not there because I didn't tell them about any of this nonsense for fear they might attend. I might not have been so willing to do what I knew must be done, if they were witnessing the disaster I had planned. Everybody was so hopeful we were going to win. Mrs. Hayter had convinced them of this. I cannot describe how great it felt to know of the ten events, we would come in dead last in at least three of them. I took great pleasure in the hearing the hopes and cheers of my classmates because I was going to crush them all.

The whistle blew, and Field Day was upon us. Let the games begin. First Event: The Wheel Barrel Race. In the wheel barrel race two people have to pair-up. One person holds the other person's feet while they walk on their hands all the way across the field. When they cross the finish line, they switch positions and then go back across the field toward the starting line. Whoever crosses the starting line first wins. I was on my hands first as the other kid held my feet. We got up into position and then, on your mark, get set, go! We took off. I was planning on making it look good at first, but the kid who was holding my feet was pulling me and preventing me from going very fast. He wanted me to look bad. Which the joke was on him because that is what I wanted, too. I finally did get across the line, and now it was time to switch.

He of course wanted to look like the hero, so he started to move very quickly. I could not abide a victory for the class, nor could I allow this asshole to be a hero. Since he felt the need to pull on my feet, I decided to push on his. I intentionally pushed them faster than he was able to walk on his hands, thereby driving his face into the gravel on the field. He just kept getting up, and I just kept driving his face into the gravel again and again. He was telling me to stop pushing so hard, and I told him I could not hear him. By the time we crossed the finish line, his face was in bad shape. He had some words for me, but he didn't do anything about it. I am proud to tell you we finished dead last. This meant nothing but a point on the board for me: Tom 1 - Class 0.

Second Event: The Frisbee Throw. This is the event our class was sure we could win. I really could throw a Frisbee. This was the easiest event to tank since it was a contest between individuals. The rest of the competitors and I lined up. One at a time, each of us would throw the Frisbee, whoever threw it the farthest won. I was the last person to throw. I was not impressed at the distance the other four competitors were able to achieve. I was certain I could beat them, but it came down to simple mathematics. I asked myself if I wanted to crush four people I did not know, or thirty people I could not stand. It was a no-brainer.

When my time came to throw, the whole crowd and all the students and parents from my class began to yell and cheer. They began to yell and scream my name. It was very loud and chaotic. For a brief moment, I thought maybe I will try to win this one thing, but I dispelled this notion and regained my sense of fair play. I threw the Frisbee no more than five feet in front of the line. I imagine many people thought I just dropped it. When the Frisbee hit the ground there was dead silence. All the yelling and screaming stopped. It was a lot like the sound of turning off a record player while it is playing. I pretended to be disappointed and went back to my group. I had my head down for two reasons. One

58

was so it looked like was disappointed, and the other was so nobody saw me trying not to laugh. I was very encouraged at this point: Tom 2 - Class 0.

The Final Event: The Tug-O-War. There were five competing classes, and there was one event left. This was the big event. The tug-o-war would count more than the other events, so it was still anybody's game. What made tug-o-war such a special event was the teachers participated in this event. Mrs. Hayter was always the anchor, which is the person at the end of the rope. The class was hopeful because Mrs. Hayter was a large woman and claimed she had never lost the tug-o-war. This is why my class was so certain of victory. They believed victory was eminent because they were of course, unaware of my intentions. Whoever won the tug-o-war would win everything. Up to this day, it was true Mrs. Hayter had never lost the tug-o-war. Somehow every kid in the fourth grade knew this. I was not too excited about breaking her perfect record, but it is as they say, "If you are going to make an omelet, you have to break some eggs."

We were up first against another class. The whistle blew and both sides started pulling. Except of course me. I could see even though I was giving no effort at all, we were still slowly winning, and this was a problem for me. I don't know what happened, but I lost my footing and fell. As I fell, I accidentally clipped the legs out from the person in front of me causing both of us to let go of the rope. This was all it took for the other team to pull the rest of us into the sand. I did not do this on purpose, but it was nevertheless a victory in my eyes. It was so loud no one heard me laughing.

We would have another chance. If we were to win the next round, we would come in third place and still get to be a part of the ice cream party. I did not care about ice cream, other than to prevent my classmates from getting it. When the next round started, I gave as equal an effort as I did in the first round. It didn't look like I was going to lose my footing, so I just had to take a dive on my own. I purposely clipped the legs out from the kid in front of me, and no one even noticed. The rest of our team got pulled into the sand as I lay on the grass laughing. The class was devastated by our second defeat in a row. We ended up finishing fifth out of five, dead last, or the worst of the worst. Tom 3 - Class 0. I win. Mission accomplished.

I felt I was the only winner in the class. I was the only one who achieved their goal. On that day, I was quite proud of what I had done. It felt good to see them upset, and I took great pride in knowing I was the reason for it. My class won every battle against me all year, only to lose the war and leave me as the only person on the battlefield who could stand tall with my head held high and a smile on my face.

My victory, as it were, was short-lived because school screwed me over. It was decided the entire fourth grade would participate in the spoils of field day. They all got ice cream. I was so pissed and disappointed about my victory dance being taken away, I could not bring myself to eat any ice cream.

Fourth grade ended. I passed.

The fifth grade was not bad at all and would prove to be my favorite year in elementary school. In the fifth grade, no one picked on me. The first day ended; then, the second day. I waited and waited, but no one ever had a harsh word for me. I even managed to make many new friends.

The only hiccup was one month into the year, we got a new person in the class, and many of the kids decided to pick on him. At first, I did not get involved. I said to myself, "Hey, I did my time. Now, it this guy's turn." I never gave this guy a hard time personally because I didn't have any interest in hurting him. It went on and on, until I couldn't take it anymore. I could not just sit there and watch the kid, who no one even knew, go through the same thing I did for so many years. I decided having friends was not worth the cost of seeing this boy suffer.

I asked my teacher, Mrs. Pemfold, to move my seat next to the new guy. She was glad to do it. The class continued to pick on him, and I took a little abuse, but it stopped completely after only just a few days. I don't know why, but the class just quit picking on him. Our class learned to get along, and it turned out to be a fantastic year. I did my work and my homework almost every day and kept my grades up all year without much of an incident. This means I was able to maintain mostly Cs and Ds with the occasional B.

I finally had finished elementary school, and I could not have been more happy to leave it all behind. I completed readiness, first, second, third, fourth and fifth grade. During these first six years of school, I learned many things. The thing I learned the most about is the thing which I am least proud. It was in elementary school where I learned how to hate. I don't get any pleasure from saying this, but from my heart, I hated those kids. This experience changed me dramatically. I was no longer the meek, mild-tempered boy I went in as. I had been tempered in the fires of ridicule. This made me tougher. I suppose some might think this was not such a bad thing. I did not see the trade-off at the time nor do I now.

I think there are more important lessons than being tough a child must learn.

I looked at my friends in the neighborhood or even my brother, Donald, and wondered how they did it. How did they go to school every year and make all these friends? I was hopeful things would change for me soon. I was hopeful I would figure out what my brother and everyone else seemed to know that I didn't. I always felt I was all alone and no one ever understood me. While I told myself every year this year would be better, I did not believe it. I was seldom wrong when I believed the worse.

I just quit caring, and I developed a real indifference toward my life. I developed an indifference toward the kids at school, and the teachers. I didn't even care about my life at home. I viewed school as something that was going to be a lifelong challenge for me. I would hear of kids getting straight As. This made no sense to me. I couldn't understand how anyone could be that perfect.

As a child I never felt more relieved than when I got my first zero on an assignment for the year. I felt relieved because I knew I could not go the whole year without a zero. I was too afraid to tank an assignment on purpose, but when it finally happened, I could relax. The first zero would rid me of my anxiety about when it was going to happen. I was more comfortable when I was failing something because the wait was over.

My indifference was not consistent. It was on and off all year long. One day I'd care, and the next day I didn't. Things were just important to me whenever they were important to me. I did not want to be the best or the worst in my class. I just wanted to be the invisible kid who no one sees or interacts with. There is no way I can explain to you what feels like to be that kid. As an adult, I understand some of my solutions were simply vengeful. I don't apologize for them; however, I realize there might have been better ways to solve these problems in the long term, but I felt there was no one I could tell and nothing I could do to change the minds of anyone. It was a no win situation for me. The only way for me to win was simply not to play, or to destroy the game.

Today, I rarely, if ever, think back this far and allow it inside my head. However, in writing about these things it has brought me back to the time when it all happened. I did not think I bore any ill will for these people. The truth is, I do. I still hate them for the way they made me feel. I hate them for the fact they used me as a stepping stone to advance themselves socially. I hate them for doing all of this at the expense of my self-esteem, a self-esteem which I went through the majority of my life without. My pain made them feel good about themselves. I don't believe I could accept their apologies today. How could they possibly be aware the level of damage they have done? They couldn't.

Chapter 5

There will never be another man in the world as awesome as my father, and there are some things I need to say on his behalf. He did an amazing job with me. He had never heard of ADD or ADHD. No one in my life had. From his point of view, I was just a kid who did not do his work. I was a kid who cared about nothing unless it interested me. I was a kid who did not apply himself while at school or while at home. It was easy for my father to believe this, as he saw my performance around the house on a daily basis, which was consistent with what I did in school. I do not fault him for anything he did or said. My brothers and I still laugh about it all today. I never doubted the love my father had for me. Never.

My ADHD was making trouble for my father and me. He did what he thought best. I do not believe any of his methods were unreasonable, and he never hit me. His methods were the methods of a loving father who wanted to see his boy succeed. The anger exhibited by my father was the exception and not the rule. When there were no problems, you never knew a sweeter, more pleasant man.

While school presented an incredible challenge for me, it was not by any means the only place things did not work in my favor. I had growing pains at home as well. I don't suppose it is too hard to understand because the math was pretty simple. If you have one workaholic father and you add a son who seemingly is living in "La La Land" and wants to do absolutely nothing, it equals chaos. Yes, life at home during this time for me had its share of chaos and drama.

I could not stand long car rides. I couldn't stand to sit anywhere for long periods of time. There were no DVDs or iPods when I was younger. The only activities we did on long trips was to count license plates on cars from other states. This just did not do it for me. We didn't take too many long family car trips. When we did, the only thing that kept me at bay was my father. I knew I would just have to deal with whatever inconvenience I was having. I knew that the world's loudest voice was only three feet in front of me.

It was Christmas break, and I will never forget the trip we took. It was the whole family in a car for twelve hours. We drove all the way from Atlanta, Georgia to Lafayette, Louisiana. Dad, Mom, Donald, Phillip and I loaded up in the car, and hit the road. I got bored before we ever cleared our own subdivision. I asked my mom, "Hey, Mom, how long does it take to get to Granny's house?"

She immediately started laughing, and my dad answered on her behalf, "Twelve hours! Do not ask again!" I did not ask again.

We left at 6:00 p.m., and we would not get there until 6:00 a.m. Dad was a burn-through-the-night kind of driver. He said we would only make one stop for gas and bathroom visits. He meant it. I guess it was around 1:00 a.m., and we were probably somewhere in Alabama. It was dark and quiet. The only sound was our car as we rode down the highway. I was sitting in the back seat with my two brothers. They were both asleep, but I was miserable sitting there with nothing to do, and no one to talk to. Then, it began.

My father smelled it first, "Ahhh! Dammit! Susan do something about this. Phil has a load in his damn diaper!" Yes, young Phillip had loaded his diaper while he was sleeping as babies do at this age. My mother grabbed little Phil, from his seat in the back and brought him into the front with her and my father. My dad wasn't really paying attention to what my mom was doing until she opened his diaper. The smell then hit us all as if it were a punch in the face, and my dad lost it.

He shouted, "Susan! What in the hell are you doing? The kid is still shitting! Let him finish shitting! It is getting all over the damned seat!" I don't know how my mom was able to laugh while smelling my little brother so close. She is the only one I ever saw laugh at my dad when he got mad.

My mother said, "Calm down. I am almost done."

I was not amused at any of this. I was bored, I couldn't sleep and all I could smell was the contents of my brother's diaper who was still sleeping. Somehow, Donald managed to sleep through the smell and my parents arguing. My mom got the diaper off little Phil and sat it next to my dad in the front seat. My dad snapped quick at my mom "Dammit, Susan! Get that away from me!"

My mother, who was still laughing, picked it up, handed it to me and said, "Here, Tommy. Take this, will you?" I was furious about having to hold Phil's diaper.

I asked, "What do you want me to do with it, Mom?"

Dad answered for her, "Dammit, Tommy, that container of shit needs to get as far away from me as it possibly can! Now, just take it and do something with it! Roll down a damn window!"

64

I looked up the road, and I could see in the distance, a speed limit sign we were coming upon. I immediately had an impulse. As I held by brother's shit-filled diaper, I thought my father was as angry as he could possibly be, which made anything I decided to do free of charge. I thought it would be fun for me to toss this diaper out the window of the moving car. My idea was to see if I could hit the sign with it. I decided to go for it.

I rolled down the window and positioned myself for the throw. The sign was getting closer and closer and then I launched my munitions at the target, and it flew out the window. BANG! It was direct hit, but it was much louder than I thought it would be. Everything went silent for a moment, but it scared the absolute hell out of my father.

Dad said, "What the hell was that, Tommy!" I did not answer him. I wanted him to forget about it, but he did not forget about it. He asked again, "Tommy! What the hell was that?"

I said, "Um...um..."

"Dammit, answer me!"

I had to tell him. "Dad, I threw Phillip's diaper at a speed limit sign." I thought my mom was going to pee in her pants laughing. She was inconsolable, laughing herself to tears. She was not laughing because she thought what I did was funny. She was laughing because she could not believe that my father had to deal with this much bullshit at one o'clock in the morning, in Alabama, while driving a car.

My dad began to yell at me, "How in the hell, are people supposed to know how fast to go when they can't read the speed limit sign through a layer of your brother's shit?"

My father's yelling went on for a good while. I wasn't really paying attention to him because I could not stop reliving the magic of the moment when Phillip's diaper hit the sign. As my father was yelling, I just kept saying "Yes, sir" every time he paused. I guess it was about twenty minutes Dad spent yelling at me. When he stopped, everything got quiet again. Everything was back to normal, just as it was before Phillip loaded his diaper. During the rest of the trip, I kept reliving my assault on the speed limit sign.

When Donald and I were around seven or eight, my mother had to take care of Phil while she ran all over the house picking up after Donald and me. Mom decided Donald and I were old enough and needed to learn how to clean up after ourselves and to pitch in around the house. Unfortunately, the job of teaching us fell upon my father.

My dad had a stronger work ethic than anybody I have ever known. Donald and I did not have a strong work ethic. We were not happy about the idea of having to work around the house in addition to school, and he had a good attitude about teaching us. We did not want to do this at first, but oddly enough, when my father explained it all to us, he made it sound as though it could be fun. When he finished explaining it all, we were okay with it. He told us he needed our help. When my father came to us with things he needed to be done, he would often come to us as if he were asking for a favor. He was soft-spoken and convincing as to his need for cooperation. I guess he just thought what he needed was going to be important to Donald and me, but it just wasn't.

Our training began with my dad having us clean our rooms. Dad went into Donald's room and my room and explained we would not be finished until our rooms were perfect and had been inspected. I can't even tell you how far from perfect our rooms were. He was very clear in what his expectations were. He showed us everything we had to do, and he even took the time to write everything down on a list for the two of us. Both Donald and I had our lists and our orders, and Dad left after telling us he would be back in an hour.

Dad also insisted that we keep our doors shut since our rooms were across the hall from each other, and Donald and I were prone to fight and argue. I don't know where that hour went, but exactly one hour later there was a knock at my door. It opened, and my dad walked into my room and could not believe what he saw.

First, the room looked exactly the same as it did an hour ago; second, I was inside one of my dresser drawers because I was trying to see if I could fit inside it. I had contorted my body in such a way that I could not see the door where my father stood. My father, realizing I could not see him, was happy to accommodate me by making use of my hearing, which was not impaired. It went something like, "Tommy! Are you insane? What in the hell are you doing, son?"

My father's thunderous voice always commanded my attention. I nearly knocked over the dresser as I managed to get myself out of the drawer. I stood up and gave him one of his favorite answers, "Nothing."

Dad said, "Yeah, I can see that! Your little brother cleaned his room, and he is going outside now! I was going to have the two of you weed the front flowerbed, but now I think I will let you do this by yourself!"

Donald was told he could go out and play, rather than work for the rest of the day. Dad then turned his attention back to me and said, "One hour, Tommy, and it better be done!" My door slammed shut behind my father; I was left standing there wondering what had just happened.

The morning this particular drama unfolded, Donald and I were watching our Saturday morning cartoons. There were three bears whose mom was putting them to bed in the drawers of a dresser, not unlike the dresser in my own room. She would tell them goodnight, kiss them and then gently push the drawer shut. We got to talking about sleeping in our drawers that night, and we both wondered if we would fit. I must have gotten obsessed with not knowing. I couldn't believe it had already been an hour, when my dad came back. I got distracted, and my curiosity became the most important thing to me. I sat in my room thinking how did I not see this coming?

Donald could not have been happier about this. He was more excited about me having to weed the flowerbed than he was about himself not being involved with it. He had this smirk on his face the whole time Dad was yelling at me. It wasn't too often he was the good son, but he was eating it up. Donald did, however, make a grave error. After he went outside, he couldn't just let it go; he had to be cute. He wanted to get all he could out of this. He came around to the side of the house to my bedroom window and started laughing at me through the glass. It didn't bother me as much as he would have liked, but it did bother me.

I walked over to the window and opened it, and we talked for a moment. I asked Donald if he wanted me to get him one of his toys out of his room and pass it through the window. He said he would and asked for one of his toys. I told him to wait a minute and left the room. Instead of getting him a toy, I went and told my dad Donald was at my window laughing at me for having to clean my room. Dad jumped up and went outside to yell at Donald.

I ran back to my room, and Donald was still there. I wanted to get there before Dad got to him, and I did. When I went back into my room, I was laughing, and when Donald saw my laughter, he knew what I had done. My father had even less patience for bullshit than he did for laziness, so Dad cancelled Donald's day of fun. Donald got shanghaied to the front yard flowerbed to pull weeds, while I finished cleaning my room.

I managed to get my room cleaned, and an hour later, my father came in to inspect it. As usual, my dad apologized for having to yell at me. He said, "Tommy, your room looks good, and I am real proud of you. Now, go out and tell your brother that you guys can take the rest of the weekend off." Donald and I got as far away from that house as we could. The problem here was not that I did not want to clean my room. Donald and I were actually looking forward to helping our dad, but the cartoon we watched was more interesting to me then cleaning my room was at the time. I had to know if I could fit in that drawer and still be comfortable enough to sleep. I couldn't let it go. I was obsessed. I could not even prioritize disappointing my father above a stupid cartoon about bears sleeping in a dresser. I did not decide to do one thing or the other, but cleaning my room never even occurred to me.

Disappointing my father always made me cry, and this was no exception. I would not have bothered worrying about the dresser if I could have seen how this would end. I just never thought it through. At the time, I was off in my own little world, and I had no idea why I was in there. During this period of distraction, I didn't think about cleaning my room one time. When my father left me the first time, I knew he was coming back, and I knew what happened when he was unhappy. The whole time he was giving directions, I could hear his words, but I was thinking about the dresser. I just was not listening to him, as was often the case when he wasn't yelling at the top of his lungs. Yelling was the only guarantee he could ever have that I would hear him. Case in point was this instance of me getting my room clean. Dad came in and yelled at me. I heard him. I cleaned my room.

At our house, Sunday was the worst day of the week for my brothers and me. In some ways, it was worse than any other day. Sunday was the day we had to get up and go to church and Sunday school. If there was one thing that Phillip, Donald and I could always agree on, it was an indifference toward going to church. It just took up so much of our day. I did not like sitting in a room for long periods of time. I did not like listening to the singing or the priest talking. I didn't like all the handshaking, the silence or the constant sitting, standing and kneeling. Sunday school, was worse than the church service. The kids in my Sunday school class were all a year older than me. Since the kids were older and bigger, they treated me like an idiot. So great, I now had people to pick on me during the weekends when the kids I went to school with weren't available.

Sundays always began the same way. My mother's sweet voice would wake us at 9:00 a.m. to tell us it was time to get ready for church. We got up, showered and put on our nice clothes. Mom would send me back upstairs to change at least once. My clothes were always wrinkled or stained. We would leave the house by about 10:30 to get there just before 11:00, which is when Sunday school started. After we finished contending with Sunday school, it was time for the service, which began at noon or whenever Father Caine decided. It would usually be around 2:00 to 2:30 before we would ever get back home.

Another thing I resented about going to church was what my dad always told us when we left.

"Have a good time at church boys, and behave." Dad did not go to church with us. He did not want to go, so he did not go. I had to give my brother Donald credit; he is the only one of the three of us who ever had the courage to ask my dad why he didn't have to go to church.

One morning Donald asked him right in front of Mom, "Hey, Dad. How come you don't ever have to go to church?" My father's head snapped toward Donald offering him no words, but he did give him something far worse. My father gave Donald "The Look". The look is a gift bestowed upon all of the Nardone men. Donald had a private chat with my father later that afternoon. I was not privy to what was said, but it never came up again.

Going to church and Sunday school was bad enough, but it was not the worst part of our Sunday. The worst part was knowing what was waiting for us back at the house. Every Sunday morning before we even left the house, Dad would inform us he was going up to the nursery to get sod, mulch, plants or whatever type of yard work paraphernalia he felt was needed to destroy our fun. This would serve to make our day that much worse than it already was. Dad told us we needed to get into yard work clothes the minute we got home. This is because in the past we would use the time we came home to figure out ways to run out the clock.

He was always so excited about yard work. I found this infuriating to see him so happy about a thing which I so loathed. His happiness and his good attitude about yard work made it very difficult for me to show my indifference towards it. It was always preferable to see my dad happy and in a good mood, but I felt yard work was an exception to this. I would have been happier if he were as pissed off as I was, and between Donald's and my shenanigans, we always managed to get him there in short order.

I can recall countless times, on the way home from church, seeing our driveway come into view from the car as my mom drove. My dad would be standing in the front yard holding a shovel or a rake. He always had this big smile on his face when we got home. It would not be long before Donald and I would fix that.

69

Donald and I never failed to piss my father off. I don't think there was a single Sunday of yard work we did not turn into a disaster. I have no idea why my father put himself through this week after week.

He used to ask us in this whiny tone, "Tommy and Donald, why does every damn Sunday have to be a damned endurance test for me?"

I asked him, "Dad, what is an endurance test?"

He just got mad and sprayed us with the hose in anger as he said, "Now get your lazy asses out of my sight." We could not have been happier to oblige him.

The reason we hated yard work was because of what my dad's idea of it was for us. He did not trust us to do anything requiring brains. Instead, he had us go to the flower bed in the front yard and pull weeds. He called it a flowerbed, but it was a weed bed. There were no flowers in it. It was just a place I now believe he allowed weeds to grow wild so he could keep us occupied while he worked and mom rested. I always resented this. Sunday yard work was almost inevitable. There were, however, three ways we could get free of it. We could get hurt; we could get in trouble for fighting or it could rain. We preferred the rain over an injury or getting into trouble, but any of the three were preferable to yard work.

Injury was rare, and even though Donald and I talked about things we could do to cause or fake an injury, we were both too afraid to risk being caught hurting ourselves. I was injured once while I was playing with the electric hedge clippers. I cut open two of my fingers. This required a bandage, but I could not work in the yard anymore that day. I kept the bandage on for a week past the time I needed it, so I could get out of yard work the following week. Dad told me I could just hold the hose, and water the azaleas. I had a big smile on my face as I watched Donald pull weeds in the dirt.

Rain was wonderful. It was as if God told us he loved us. One Sunday, while on the way home from church, we received an amazing gift. It began to rain. This canceled my dad's plans for a huge day of yard work and saved the weekend for Donald and me. We could not have been more thrilled about this. I was so excited I shared something with my mother on the way home.

I said to my mother, "Mom, this is amazing! When I was in church today, I prayed for it to rain on the way home!" Donald and I did this every Sunday. When we got home, my dad was not out front. He was sitting in his chair watching television with a sad look on his face. I was sorry my dad was disappointed but not sorry enough to pray for the rain to stop.

I could see my dad was upset about the weather ruining his plans. I actually went to him, while he was sitting in his chair and said, "Dad, I am sorry it is raining."

My mom shot right back with a laugh and said, "Oh, the hell you're sorry! You told me in the car you were praying for it to rain today at church." I would rather if she had not said this in front of my dad. Upon hearing this, my dad gave me "The Look". I just quietly walked away hoping he would not yell or find something else for me to do.

Fighting was a sure fire way for Donald and I to find ourselves sprayed with the hose and sent to bed without dinner. Donald and I fighting always drove my father crazy. Dad could not stand to see us fight with each other. He would almost always lose his cool and shout and yell. There were many times my brother and I just got along out of fear of my dad raising hell.

I recall one time when Donald and I were sitting on the floor playing records. We began to fight with each other over whose turn it was. We did not realize our father was home until we noticed him standing in the doorway. Donald and I felt quite comfortable. Upon noticing him, there was a dead silence between us. Dad broke the silence by asking us in a very calm tone of voice, "Boys, what are you fighting about?" I blamed Donald, and Donald blamed me. Dad said "Oh, wait, wait. I have the solution to this," and then he began violently stomping his foot down smashing a perfectly good record player to bits, while wearing his black leather shoes. Donald and I sat there only twelve inches from the destruction as this was going on. We watched in horror, as it became little pieces of broken plastic. When the record player was destroyed to my father's satisfaction, he just said in a still calm voice, "There, now you don't have anything to fight about. Why don't you boys go out and play?" He never even raised his voice.

Donald and I skipped Sunday school one day and were hanging out in the woods next to the church. My mom wasn't there because she was sick at home, but she asked our neighbor to take us. It was really hot and the subject of yard work came up in our conversation. I had this idea and I ran it by Donald and he loved it. We were actually excited about it. We decided we would get out of yard work by staging a fight.

We knew if there was one thing we could do to get my father's attention, it was to fight. Donald and I got home, changed our clothes and went outside to our post in the front flower bed. Twenty minutes into it, I threw some dirt at Donald. Donald began yelling at me and smacked me with a clump of weeds. We both started wrestling in the flower bed and just as expected, Dad came over with hose in hand and shouted as only he could, "What in the hell are you two morons doing?" I told Dad that Donald threw dirt at me, and Donald came right back and told him that I threw dirt at him first. Dad very calmly asked me, "Tommy, did you throw dirt at your brother?"

I said, "Yes, sir."

Dad, calmly, asked Donald, "Donald, did you throw dirt at your brother?"

He answered him, "Yes, sir."

My father stepped toward us and sprayed us both with the hose. We were too afraid to move out of the water path. When my father was finished spraying us down, he pointed and yelled as we ran into the house, "You two get your stupid asses inside! I can't believe you can't even get through a single day of work without being assholes to each other! Oh, and unh-uh boys, guess what's for dinner. ...Nothing, and you can have as much as you want of it!"

This happened often, but this was the first time we had ever staged it. I remember feeling bad at first, but in the end, it was worth it. It was somewhat cool that my brother and I worked together on something. There were not too many times that we helped each other to get something that we both wanted so badly. Phil for some reason was not as lazy as my brother and I were. He used to get excited about us finishing and actually tried to pull all the weeds out of the garden.

The hope of any type of work ever being canceled was thrilling to me. Going to bed at three o'clock in the afternoon with no supper was actually preferable to working in the flower bed for two hours. It did not matter what the job was. I did not want to do anything ever.

Then, my father taught me to cut the grass. He was very leery of me doing anything requiring me to think or anything dangerous. I had not convinced him I had the ability to think. Learning to cut the grass was fun the first couple of times, but I got bored with it very quickly.

I was very angry one day when my brother and I were going to ride our bikes. We got outside and my dad said, "Hey, Tommy, I need you to cut the grass for me, buddy." My day was now completely shot because I now had to spend an hour of it working. I was furious, but I didn't let my dad know it. I got the mower, filled it up with gas, took it to the front yard and started it up.

I was so angry as I started mowing the lawn. My brother Donald was loving it. He did not even go anywhere. He sat on his bike next to my dad, and they both watched me cut the grass. Donald did not enjoy watching me do things unless it was something I didn't want to do. I was about ten minutes into the one-hour job. Then, as a gift from God, the lawn mower seized up and shut off.

Apparently, since my dad handed over the responsibility of the cutting the grass to me, he neglected to make sure the lawn mower had oil in it. When it finally ran out of oil, the engine just locked up. I was absolutely thrilled. I pushed that crappy yellow lawnmower down the front yard and into the garage where my dad was. He could see the excitement in my face when I told him the lawnmower broke. I said it in a way he knew it pleased me.

This pissed him off immediately. Dad said, "Donald, get me my damn drill quick!" Donald quickly moved with a purpose. He wanted the lawnmower fixed as bad as my father did. My father in no time had the top off the engine. He first topped it off the oil level, and then he hooked one of his largest sockets up to his drill and placed it on top of the motor and forced the mower to start turning until once again the mower was running as if nothing ever happened. Donald looked at me and started laughing. My dad looked at me, but he was not laughing.

Dad saw the disappointment in my face at his quick victory over the lawnmower. He said, "Donald, son, you best get on your bike and go play. Your brother is going to be busy for a while because I am going to work the lazy out of his ass!" Donald laughed as he rode away on his bike. I am sure he couldn't wait to tell all of our friends about the current events going on in my life.

A similar thing happened with a vacuum cleaner one time, except it was the belt that broke. I was pretty excited when this happened too, but I made sure to pretend to be pissed about it. When the vacuum broke, I was loving it. I just knew I was done vacuuming for the day, but wouldn't you know my dad had an extra belt. It wasn't two minutes until it was back in my hands.

I freely admit I was lazy. I did not ever want to work, but there is a little more to it. I would get my mind ready for one thing and when I was told to do another, I just could not allow myself to let go of my former thoughts. I found many things to be boring, and I could not stand to be bored. When I was bored, I got angry and irritable. What Dad had us do every week was just simple grunt work. When I became older and was told to cut the grass, there were no problems until I got bored with cutting the grass. I was not able to stand or sit still as a child. I needed something to engage my mind. I could never do anything in which I had no interest.

Chapter 6

I told myself the sixth grade was going to be just as smooth as the fifth grade. I was afraid of the new school and the expectations of me now that I was in middle school. My indifference was briefly cast aside, as a result of my success in the fifth grade. This new attitude of mine would not even last through the end of the first school day.

In the sixth grade I would face the two meanest teachers that Hell ever belched from its bowels. Mrs. Tempest and Mrs. Durfee were their names. They were both a completely different kind of teacher.

They were hateful all the time, and they only smiled when they were making somebody's life difficult. Mrs. Durfee did not give me near as much trouble as Mrs. Tempest, but she seemed to enjoy it more. She was always delighted when informing me of my zeroes whereas Mrs. Tempest liked to yell about it. It was the perfect evil marriage with those two, and they were as thick as thieves.

I wanted to do well in the sixth grade, and I began with a good attitude. I knew it would be more work, and perhaps harder work, but I did not want to allow middle school to be a repeat of all the things I did wrong in elementary school. I really wanted middle school to be a turning point for me. As it happened, it was.

On the first day of sixth grade, I was in Mrs. Tempest's class, and she was giving instructions for the assignment on which we were to work. Just like old times, I came out of my daydream and had no idea what I was to be working on. I thought I would just take the zero to avoid embarrassment, but I could not go through another year as I did in the fourth grade. I decided I would just have to ask Mrs. Tempest what we were supposed to be doing. It took a lot of courage for me to get up, walk across the classroom and ask her a question. I decided I would do it.

I quietly got up and went to Mrs. Tempest while she sat at her desk. When I got there, I asked her to repeat the assignment. She looked at me as if I owed her money. She stood up and while pointing at my empty seat, she disrupted the entire class as she began shouting at me. "Mr. Nardone! I spent ten minutes explaining the assignment to the whole class. If you don't know what to do, then that is just too bad! Now, go sit down and be quiet!"

It took all the nerve I had in me to get up and walk across the room of people who were not my friends and ask her for directions. She could have just answered me. She could have just kept her voice down. She could have just pointed to my desk as her own quiet refusal and still maintained her credibility as a spiteful bitch, but no. Mrs. Tempest was hell-bent on making life a living hell for all of her students. The same exact thing happened to me with Mrs. Durfee the same week.

It made me afraid of my own teachers. They caused and validated the class's decision to make me the butt of every joke for the rest of the year, and they taught me the stupidest thing I could do was to think that they were there to help me. They taught me the price for my inability to pay attention would be ridicule and scorn from my teachers and my classmates. I was sure I would never ask either of them another question ever again. I felt a zero was a much better outcome than communicating with them.

For the next five weeks, I had trouble paying attention and listening to instructions. I would miss assignments and not make them up. I didn't even know if I was allowed to make up my work. I did not ask because it was not worth going through the drama I felt was certain. I received zero after zero, and soon enough I occurred to me: I was back in the same place I found myself in the fourth grade. I quit caring and quit trying. I knew there was no way I would ever pull myself out of this hole, so why bother putting forth an effort? I knew my report card would be awful, but I just put it out of my mind.

The day came to receive my first report card for my sixth grade year. I always thought optimistically on the weekend prior to this day. On the way to school, I thought surely I had to have done well in at least one class. I eventually had myself thinking I had done something well enough to warrant a D or even a C. I had not even gotten my report card, and I was taking myself through the steps of the grieving process.

The morning of report card day, as I rode the bus, I was in denial as I actually thought, *Maybe my teachers would make a mistake, and accidentally give me a better grade than what I deserved*, or *Maybe they will develop a conscience and feel sorry for me and award me a D.* By the time I got to school, I truly believed these things.

When I got off the bus and walked to classroom, reality began to set in. Mrs. Tempest passed out the report cards to the class. I tried again to think of any possible way I might have done well in even one single class, but I could not. I tried to recall one assignment I did for which I received a good grade, but I could not. As bad as I might have thought I had done, I was not prepared for what this itemized sum of my efforts would reveal.

Mrs. Tempest came to my desk, looked at me and just shook her head in disappointment as she placed an envelope with my name on it in the center of my empty desktop. I picked up the envelope and opened it quickly as a final dash of hope ran through my mind. All I had was hope, but hope was not enough.

The report card I received is the report card nobody ever gets. My report card was the absolute benchmark for failure. My report card was an example of the report card that allows people to save face and not be discouraged as they say, "Well, at least I didn't get all Fs." Yes, I got all Fs. I earned an F in all of my classes. I didn't do well enough in any subject for which any teacher felt I was even worthy of a D. This was my report card: straight Fs.

I was catatonic. I went past anxiety, past sadness, past anger, past fear. I was catatonic. I was not even aware it was possible to achieve such a milestone in failure. As far as I knew I was the one in my class who managed to break the glass floor and open this option for the rest of the world.

There was a redneck in my class, whose speech was so bad, I could barely understand him. He was always squinting, and I remember thinking that he always looked like he was confused. This complete moron, academically speaking, had done better by receiving two Ds. My report card could have actually made him feel better about himself. As if I did not feel bad enough, I watched the dumbest son of a bitch in the room take home a better report card than me.

We always got our report cards, first thing on a Monday morning. This was not the best way I could imagine starting my day or the week. I spent the rest of the day walking around from class to class as the bells rang one after another bringing me ever closer to the day's end. This day went very quickly. I felt this strange fog surrounding me all day, as I went through the motions of changing classes. I did not even see a need to get the books out of my locker. I went from class to class with nothing but this crappy report card in my hand. I would just stare at it. I was still trying to process how this was possible, but I could not grasp it. I was looking at it, and I still had not accepted it. I could not get myself to believe it.

Throughout the day, I would notice people as they were talking about their own report cards. I suspect that most of them had done a little better than I had. I spent the day wondering if anyone else in the entire school got straight Fs. I thought about the fact that there was no possibility a single person in the school could have done worse than I did. It just wasn't possible mathematically.

During my lunch period, I entered the cafeteria, bought my lunch, sat down and began staring at my food. I sat there in silence for a moment until it was interrupted when I heard a girl crying. I looked over and saw this girl as she was in tears. Her friend was consoling her. I thought, *Hey, maybe her pain can ease mine.* As I continued to eavesdrop, I was encouraged further to see she was upset about her report card.

I heard her friend as she said, "Don't cry, it's only a B." I immediately lost interest and just let their foolishness wash right over me without giving it another thought.

Eventually it was time for the last bell. It rang, and I went out to my bus. I got on the bus and sat down where a couple of my friends from my neighborhood were. They inquired about my report card, and said, "I'll bet you did better than me."

My response was "I will bet you five thousand dollars I didn't." With that, I handed him my report card. He looked at it in amazement and passed it to someone else. My report card began to make its way around the bus. I thought to get up and get it back, but I realized how good it seemed to be making everyone else feel, so I just let it go. If it were to get lost, it's not as if I would have had trouble recalling my grades. Who would lie, and say they got all Fs? Eventually I did get it back. My friend handed it to me and said, "Wow, Tommy. I sure am sorry, man." I just said, "Ehh."

While still in a catatonic type of depression I got off the bus and walked home. I got home to an empty house as my parents were not home from work yet. Donald and Phillip got home an hour later. Donald was in the fifth grade, and Phillip was in the first grade. I was sitting in silence on the couch without the TV on when my brothers got home. Phil came running up to me and said, "Tommy, look at my report card. I got all smiley faces." I looked at him without a word and smiled as best as I could.

Donald was very angry. He got a bad report card as well. He said, "Tommy, look at this. Dad is going to kill me." I assured my brother, anything Dad had to say to him would most likely be quick, so that he could get to me. Donald stopped and said, "Oh, shit. Let me see your report card, brother."

I pulled it out and handed it to him. I thought Donald would never stop laughing. It was like one of those funny pictures you see and laugh at, and then, just when you stop laughing, you look at it again, and it is just as funny as the first time you saw it. I sat there and watched my brother laugh at my failings, and I did not even care enough to look in his direction as he literally rolled on the floor.

One might have thought I was a little scared or nervous about bringing this report card home to my father. I wasn't. I knew my dad, and I knew he would just yell and raise hell at me for being lazy until he got tired. I had seen this show a thousand times. One might also have thought I was a little scared or nervous about bringing this report card home to my mother, who was a schoolteacher, but I wasn't. I knew my mom would just yell and scream believing I was a smart boy and say I just didn't give a shit.

I was not afraid of anything. I had taken my game to ground zero. My report card could be equated to a gold medal in the Disappointment Olympic Games. I had nothing of which to be afraid. I knew my next report card wouldn't be any worse because how could it be? I had no fear. I probably could have walked through hell, stared the devil in the face and given him the finger. I had reached the bottom and no matter how little I did in school from here on out, I would not be in any worse shape. In fact, if I were to go back to school the next day and earn a D on any assignment, my grade mathematically would improve. I could do no worse. There were no more degrees of failure. I had hit bottom.

There was another, far bigger reason I was not scared. I was genuinely just curious how my parents would react. I normally brought home a bad report cards, this was nothing new. I would sit on the hearth of the fireplace and watch them both. They were like a yelling tag team. They would just go back and forth taking turns yelling. While it was happening, I would at some point quit listening and revert to counting the bricks on the hearth of the fireplace where I sat. Sometimes while they were yelling I would just stare at them both and note how physically exhausted the two of them had become from yelling for three hours and try to guess what time it would end. I knew they loved me. You really have to love someone to care enough to yell for three straight hours. This takes a great deal of energy.

This was a completely different thing. I had no idea what was in store for me, and to be honest, the anticipation was killing me. I knew I was only an hour away from the "Big Show". In a very twisted way, the anticipation of wondering what my parents would say oddly caused me to look forward to it a little.

I went to my room and began packing up all of my things. I knew this was going to happen anyway, so why not just get the jump on it. I knew what to pack up. I packed up anything that made me happy and put it in the same box I packed the last time. I sat in my room playing reruns of the last time my father did not like my report card. As I was sitting there waiting for my dad to get home, I wondered which of his catch phrases would be used first.

Donald was so excited to hear what my dad would say to me he was no longer worried about his own bad report card. He came in and asked me, "What are you going to say, Tommy?"

I said, "Nothing."

Eventually I heard the unmistakable sound of my dad's car pulling up in the driveway. Phillip couldn't wait to show Dad his report card. My father came in and was very pleased to see all smiley faces. He gave Phil a hug and said, "That is a good boy, Phillip." He then gave him one of his coveted head rubs. Dad did this occasionally when he was proud of us. My mom came home in the middle of Phil's head rub, and she too was very proud of young Phillip.

I knew it was going to happen soon enough, and then, it did. My dad yelled back for us. He seemed to be in a very good mood thanks to Phillip. He shouted, "Tommy and Donald, come on in the den."

It was show time. It was time, once again, to ruin my parent's evening and destroy any hopes they might have about my adjusting to the new school. My dad happily and jokingly said, "Hey, boys! Let's see 'em."

Mom said, "Okay, who is first?"

I explained, it would probably be best, if Donald went first. They saw Donald's report card, and they were not happy at all. They began with the questions. Donald did not have any of the right answers. Mom and Dad began to yell at Donald and just as they were about to hit their stride, Donald blurted out with a display of strategically brilliant timing, "Well, Tommy got all Fs!" The house went silent.

Now, I had to hand it to Donald. I was not very happy with him for blurting this out, but I later saw the genius of this outburst. He stopped the attention to his own failings by selling me down the river. I really wasn't mad since they were going to find out eventually. I would have done the same thing to him.

The silence following Donald's remark was a very eerie silence. My parents looked at me, and Dad said, "Tommy... is this true?" I said nothing, I just handed the report card to him as I stared at the floor. He was shocked and said nothing. He gestured to my mom to look at it with him as if he was without the ability to interpret its meaning, but my mother was not even sure. No one spoke. They were also a little bit catatonic as their reaction was not unlike my own upon seeing this for

80

the first time. They stared at it as if they couldn't read English and were trying to sound out the letters. My dad looked at Donald and calmly said, "Donald... get out." Donald left.

My mother did not say a word. She just began crying and then she left the room. It was not easy to watch my mother cry in response to my report card. My dad did not yell. He just looked at it and asked me to explain. I gave him his least favorite answer in the whole world. I said to him, "I don't know."

He spoke to me about all the ways my life was about to change. He spoke of things I enjoyed doing with a very pleasant and happy voice only to quickly say, "That is over." He would list all the things I enjoyed about being alive and then say, "That is over."

He spent twenty minutes calmly explaining this to me and closed with this final thought that caused his voice to gradually elevate in tone and volume, "Now, go into your shit-pit of a room and pack up everything you enjoy in a box. The only thing you have any time for now is books. Welcome back, prisoner!"

I thought I could impress him a little bit by telling him I already had the things in my room packed. I said, "They are already packed."

He just said, "Good! Now get the hell out of my sight!" I felt a little slighted he did not even seem impressed I had already packed up my fun stuff.

I walked back to my room and began to cry. I was sad I disappointed my father again, and I no longer believed I would ever again make him proud the way I did when I was younger.

I didn't go outside, and I did not watch TV. I brought all my books home every day, and I was to study the whole day. I also studied on the weekends. I once again got to where I didn't even care whether I was at school or not. The weekends were just as bad as the weekdays, and my grades were not getting much better. Things sucked at school, and things sucked home.

My dad was not a bastard. He really thought I was being lazy and not doing the work. I suppose there was some truth his thinking. In spite of my father's strict enforcement of my restriction, there was a weekend he felt sorry for me and said, "Hey, Tommy, why don't you go outside this weekend and play with your friends? They probably miss you, buddy." I just told him I was going to go to my room and study. I thanked him and walked back to my room and closed the door. It was true. I didn't want to go out and play with my friends because I just didn't care anymore. I had been on restriction for almost six weeks, and I did not care if I ever got off. I was not expecting my next report card to be too much better than the last one.

My next report card came in, and it was a little better. I managed to pull three of my grades up to a D. Yes, the coveted D, the absolute beginning of mediocrity. It was all I ever wanted. Hoping for more would have just seemed greedy. I went through the day and got home. Phil got his smiley faces again, and Donald somehow managed to pull himself out of the mire, but not me. My dad looked at my report card, let out a big disappointing sigh and said, "Well, prisoner, I sure do hope you like the sixth grade because it looks like you are committed to going through it twice." I was of course, still on restriction and forced to stay in the house and do more studying.

My mom came back and wanted to talk to me. She begged me to tell her why I was doing so poorly. There actually was a reason for some of this. I had not discussed it with my parents. I never even asked my teachers about it because it was sure to result in them embarrassing me in front of the class. I knew my parents would not believe it because it was too ridiculous. It was exactly the type of thing a young sixth grader would make up to protect his ass, but I figured "what the hell" and I told her. I explained to my mother when we take all our tests and quizzes, we switch papers and grade our neighbor's test. I explained further that Mrs. Tempest has a policy if the person grading your test doesn't put their initials on it, you receive a zero on your test.

My mom said, "Now, Tommy. That is just silly."

I said, "Mom, I agree." My mom was of course referring to the validity of my story and not Mrs. Tempest's policy. She did not believe me when I told her this was actually happening. She explained to me that a teacher could not do this.

I said, "Okay, Mom."

She asked again why I was failing, and I said, "Mom, I don't want to tell you again. You don't believe me, so what can I do? Do you want me to lie to you?"

Mom was convinced I was lying and scheduled a parent-teacher conference. I was glad. My mom told me every day leading up to this conference a teacher would never do this. She would give me an opportunity each day to confess this lie before it was too late. I just responded, "You will see, Mom." The conference was coming soon, and I could not wait to hear my mom rip into Mrs. Tempest.

When we arrived at Mrs. Tempest's room, my mother and father introduced themselves. My mother began almost immediately with her question. Mrs. Tempest confirmed what my mother refused to believe. My mother's jaw dropped when she heard it come out of Mrs. Tempest's mouth. I eventually tuned out during their arguing. I was looking around the room. I was in another world. I don't know how much later it was in the conversation, but they wanted me to participate.

Mrs. Tempest said to me, "Tommy, you have not turned in assignments for the last two weeks. Don't you think that has something to do with what caused your failing grades?"

My response was "Well, of course it does, but if Wes Walker does not initial my test when he grades it, then I get a zero and fail anyway so what difference does it make?" There was silence.

I thought, *Oh to hell with it,* and I brought up the way she let the class treat me, and the way she yelled at me when I asked her a question. I started to cry, but then, Mrs. Tempest started to cry. When I saw her tears, I turned to stone. What was sadness a moment ago turned to fury.

I thought, *How dare this woman cause all of this and then try to masquerade as someone with a conscience?* My parents asked me to go into another room and wait for a bit. They talked a while. I had no idea about what. I never even cared enough to ask. They called me back in and, apparently, decided things would be a little different. It seemed everything was resolved.

Mrs. Tempest and my parents decided it would be best to fix all my grades for which I had been given zeroes due to her ridiculous rule. Mrs. Tempest said, "I am sorry that things have been so bad, Tommy," and then she started crying again.

While crying, she asked me, "Could I have a hug?"

I told her, "NO! You cannot!"

My father shouted, "Tommy!" I would never defy my father, but I would have rather been be kicked in the nuts, then to show this woman any affection or to give her the slightest reason to think any of this was okay with me. My mom began to cry again, so I put on a show to end the drama. I hugged Mrs. Tempest; we left and went home.

There was not a word spoken on the way home. My mom felt bad for not believing me, but who could blame her? My father was the only person who was seemingly in a good mood, and when we got home, I found out why. Dad came back to my room and said, "Tommy, I knew you weren't lying. You have never lied to me. Don't worry, bud, we are going to get past all this." He was right; we did.

It didn't take long for me to hate my middle school. I managed to squeak by the sixth grade, and I passed barely with a D average. I was happy with that. By this time in my life, school was not about learning; it was about not failing and just going to the next grade. All I cared about was getting finished with it. I did not care how. It was in the sixth grade where I realized I only wanted to do the bare minimum. I was jaded and bitter about my life. I just wanted to do what I had to do to keep my parents and my teachers quiet.

Chapter 7

On the first day of the seventh grade. The teacher I hated more than all the other teachers I ever had moved from the sixth grade to the seventh grade, and she would be my science teacher. She had a big smile on her face when she saw me come into her class for the first time. I could not believe it. I just wanted to die. I knew right away the seventh grade was going to be just as big a turd as the sixth. She spoke first, "Good morning, Tommy."

To which I replied, "Good morning, Mrs. Tempest."

One thing made the seventh grade better than the sixth grade was having many different teachers and different classes for each subject. Most of my fellow students only saw me one time per day for about an hour. The bullies did not have enough time to figure out enough about me to make fun. It eventually did happen, of course, but not the daily dose that I was accustomed to. Most of what I heard was about my acne, and it really bothered me.

The seventh grade was a special year for me. It was the year I met the greatest teacher I ever had; Mrs. Chambers. I loved that lady. She was never anything to me but helpful, kind and considerate. I was fortunate enough to have her for two classes, math and English. One of the coolest things about Mrs. Chambers was she was also not a huge fan of Mrs. Tempest. She never said it aloud, but I just knew.

Math and English were the two most difficult classes of my sixth grade year. This was in no small part due to my unwillingness to pay the price for asking questions of the teachers. I had to go home and figure it out myself using the textbook with the example problems in my textbook.

Mrs. Chambers was an entirely different kind of teacher. One thing was clear to me from the beginning: She enjoyed what she did. She really seemed to enjoy teaching, and she was incredibly entertaining. Mrs. Chambers was funny and not in a way other teachers were. She had a very unique sense of humor. I listened to her every day, and I would hang on her every word. I never had trouble in her class. The other thing about Mrs. Chambers is she would not put up with any shenanigans. Nobody ever gave Mrs. Chambers a hard time, and more importantly, nobody gave me a hard time in her class, not ever.

One thing Mrs. Chambers told us on the first day of school in her English class was we were to keep a journal. She wanted us to write at least two pages, and turn it in every Friday. She did not care about what we wrote. She told us to write whatever we wanted, she would not discuss it with anyone. I remember being intrigued by this assignment. I did not like the idea of having to write two whole pages every week, but it counted forty percent of our grade, so I did it.

I began my journal the following day. I put Mrs. Chamber's promise of confidentiality to the test. I wrote about my week at school. I wrote about every terrible thing anyone said to me, and I wrote about a big confrontation I had with Mrs. Tempest. She did not believe something I told her, and she was making a huge deal out of it. My journal was a record of all the things that went on in my life at school throughout the week. I even used whatever curse words I felt I needed to make my point. I enjoyed writing in my journal very much.

Friday came and half the class had completely forgotten about their journals. I didn't. She came around and picked them up. I exceeded the two-page minimum, and I remember feeling like an overachiever. I almost did not turn it in because I worried about the backlash from the things I had said, and the way I said them. I did not give my journal another thought until she was passing them back to us on Monday morning.

I was anxious to find out what she thought, while also scared at the trouble I might find myself in. She went down the desks row by row handing each journal back one kid at a time. The anticipation was killing me. Finally, she got to me, and said in a stern voice, "Mr. Nardone?"

"Yes?" I said.

She said, "See me after class, please."

I said, "Yes ma'am."

I spent the whole class thinking how foolish it was to write an assignment and not only use words like *shit, damn* and *hell* in it, but I actually referred to Mrs. Tempest as an "evil bitch". I just knew that I had gone too far. The bell rang, and the class got up to leave. I slowly walked up to Mrs. Chambers' desk staring at the floor, and said, "Mrs. Chambers, I am sorry. I should not have used that kind of language in my journal. I should not have called Mrs. Tempest that name. I understand if I am in trouble."

She sat there with a giant grin on her face and waited for me to look at her. When I did, she broke out in an uncontrollable laughter that I could not even believe.

She said, "Mr. Nardone, I was reading all of these journals last night, and I was so bored that I thought I should have my head examined for creating such an assignment. The journals I read were the most boring I have ever seen, until I got to yours." She went on and on about how great my writing was, and how she could not stop laughing. At the end, she did say for the future, she would prefer if I did not use bad language. I said sure. From that day forward, I believed Mrs. Chambers and I were best friends.

The worst class I had to take in the seventh grade was P.E. Most people really liked it, but one kid's "Physical Education" was this kid's "Physical Exertion", and I just did not want any part of it. What made it harder this year was the entire PE department was so excited that their department was finally being deemed relevant on a national level.

It was "President Reagan's Physical Fitness Challenge". I remember hearing the principal on the morning announcements saying how he wanted every kid in the school to pass this. He seemed sure that everybody at Caineville Middle School would be able to achieve this milestone of self-improvement. I guess that is what he said because the only thing I heard was "blah blah blah". I had no interest in anything my school was involved in, particularly those things taking place in the gymnasium.

I was not going to submit to this nonsense. I had enough to do in the classroom and at home. I refused to make any of this a priority. My coach's name was Coach Reyner. He did not like me very much. I can't blame him. One day while doing the roll call, I was looking at this pretty girl in my class. Given my age, things suddenly became very hard on me, and the coach asked me to get up and do something for him. I was wearing sweat pants and I knew that the consequences for defying him would be preferable to the consequences of standing up in a gym with a hundred other kids, while I walked across the floor sporting a boner. I just looked at him and said, "No, coach."

He said, "Okay," and made a check mark in his book. I got after school detention for three days, but I made a new friend who thought I was a bad-ass for refusing to do a favor for the coach.

It came time for the fitness test, and I still just didn't care. I was so indifferent to the school for having these expectations of me. I purposely tanked the exam. One part of the test involved us doing as many sit-ups as we could do in sixty seconds. I didn't like my school or

Coach Reyner, so I did not care to impress any of them by doing well. I knew my parents weren't going to give a damn how many sit-ups I did in PE class.

At the exam, each of us had to pair up with another student. My new friend and I paired up, and he went first. I held his feet, and he gave it everything he had. He did over seventy sit-ups. I was very impressed. The coach called out the names and the holder (that was me) would call out the number of sit-ups they did in the sixty seconds we were allotted. The coach called my partner's name, and I proudly said, "Seventy-four." As it turns out that was about the average number for the jock types that were there.

Then, it was time to switch. My holder said to me, "Okay, Tom. Let's knock this out. You can do it!"

To which I sarcastically responded, "Uh yeah, you just watch my smoke."

I did one sit-up and then decided, *That is all they get.* I relaxed on my back for the remaining time we were given to complete the test. When it was time to call the numbers, my partner asked, "Tommy, do you really want me to say one?" I told him, "Of course I do."

When the coach said, out loud, "Nardone", my partner replied, "One." The coach slammed down the clipboard and looked at me. The whole gym was laughing and looking at me.

The coach said from the table, "Nardone, are you telling me one sit-up is the best you can do? Are you telling me you couldn't even squeeze out two sit-ups?"

I replied, "Of course I could have done two sit-ups, but I still would have failed."

Coach said, "Okay, Nardone, do you want to try this again or do you want me to send this report to the President of the United States of America that says Tommy Nardone can't do more than one sit-up?"

I asked, "Do you think he will be disappointed in me?" The coach just rolled his eyes and continued down the list.

In spite of the fact that I let down and shamed my coach, my school and my country, I did pass most of my classes that year. Having Mrs. Chambers as one of my teachers made the ridicule not seem to matter so much. I did not even dread going to school because Mrs. Chambers' classes were the first and last classes of my day. The seventh grade ended, and I had only one more year to go in middle school.

I was nervous about going on to the eighth grade. I was very intimidated as I thought it was going to be far more difficult than the seventh or the sixth grades. I was not wrong. It was going to be another year of chaos and disappointments. I began to mentally prepare for the worst.

In the eighth grade, I had real trouble with my grades. This was mostly to do with a teacher named Mrs. Borden. Her class was harder than Mrs. Tempest's class ever was. The main difference with her was she was very sarcastic about questions I asked her. She was not as mean as Mrs. Tempest, but she really seemed to enjoy making me feel stupid. The only people she cared about were all of the popular kids. She treated me almost as bad as they did.

Mrs. Borden was my English teacher. She had us reading all the time and taking tests on what we read. I had trouble with reading comprehension. It was not just short stories with Mrs. Borden; she had us read actual books. I didn't read any of the books I was asked to read.

It was not because I was lazy, I just couldn't figure out how to silence my brain long enough to read a story. I couldn't keep any of the characters straight in my head. I read two or three pages, and then I stopped to review what had happened. I asked myself, "Now, what has happened so far?" I did not know.

I often forget what story we were to read, or I forgot we had to read one at all. While riding the bus to school in the morning, not having read my story, I read every other paragraph or every other page of the story. It never worked. I always scored low. It did not matter if I read the story or not. I would still fail the tests. I did not get straight Fs, but I did not do well enough to avoid restriction. I got two Fs and four Ds.

If it wasn't for a girl in my class who felt sorry for me, I don't know how I would have passed. She and I came up with a system of taps she could use to indicate to me what the answers on the quizzes were. Eight taps on the desk with her pencil meant number eight. She would tap on my foot with her foot one to four times signaling A, B, C or D. I really cannot imagine how I would have passed the eighth grade had it not been for the willingness of this girl to help me cheat.

One of the Fs was in PE. I did not want to play dodge ball, so I sat on the bleachers and talked to the other derelicts who did not care about getting their workout in before their next class. Dad raised hell, so I had to start playing dodge ball. I hated dodge ball. I also did not care much for Coach Reyner. He was overweight, but somehow felt it was his mission in life to get me and the rest of the class into shape.

Of all the teachers who gave me an F, Coach Reyner was the only one who seemed pleased to do it. He had a happy, smug look on his face. My father told me I could not get any Fs. I was going to have to play dodge ball to appease him. The next day at school I went out on the basketball court with all the other kids, and got my ass kicked. To them I was fresh meat.

This thing between Coach Reyner and me became very personal to me. He knew his giving me an F caused me to have to join the crowd. He watched me for the whole class period and appeared to be smiling or laughing every time I went down. I did not like him laughing at me as if he had won. I decided I could not and would not abide his victory stare for one more day.

The thought of his defeat appeared to me as vividly as the kite did so many years ago. Only this kite, I was going to take control of it. I saw myself controlling this situation and steering it as I saw fit. I was going to control the altitude. I was going to control the speed. I was going to see this through. This kite consumed my attention, and I was willing to spend all the energy I had chasing it until it was caught.

I was smaller than most of the kids, and all the bigger kids liked to throw the ball at the smaller kids to see if they could knock them down. I was not about to be involved in that foolishness. The first day playing dodge ball, I was the target for all the big kids, and they really wanted a piece of me since I had avoided them for the past six weeks. They were merciless in their attempt to throw that big red ball at me, and it hurt like hell. I would watch Coach Reyner laughing and smiling every time that ball knocked me down. I decided his amusement came at too great a cost. I decided I was going to win. I knew after class ended, I would never again be the object of his entertainment. Coach Reyner must be stopped.

I thought long and hard about this particular dilemma. I knew to pass P.E. I would need to please Coach Reyner or have him somehow allow me to sit on the bleachers. I knew the path of submission would offer the least resistance, but that path never appealed to me. I determined I would have to make my involvement in the game a bigger pain in the ass for him than my lack of involvement. I developed my plan, and I could not wait to execute it and wipe that smile off his face.

The next day when I walked into gym class, I went right up to him and humbly said, "Coach, I want to apologize to you. I am sorry for all the days I have not been participating in your class. I have shown you great disrespect, and I am sorry. I also want to thank you. Yesterday, while I was playing out there I think I learned a lot about myself and the things I can do."

Coach Reyner was quite surprised, and he gave me a double take as he said, "Well, Nardone, that is very mature of you to come up here like a man and admit this to me. I forgive you, Nardone, and I am glad you came to me. That is what this is all about, becoming an adult. I am looking forward to seeing you out there."

I said, "Thanks, coach. I am looking forward to being out there." I could not believe he bought it. He was actually proud of himself. I imagine he must have felt as if he had gotten through to me. All he did was motivate me to see this through to certain victory.

I went to the locker room and changed into my gym shorts. I came out of the locker room and went to my position on the floor. Everybody always yelled when the first match began. I made sure I was near Coach Reyner, so when the yelling began, he would see me excited about some dodge ball. I was right there yelling with all the other jock, wannabe, douche bag rednecks. He even gave me the thumbs up. I was laughing at him, but he thought I was just happy to be bettering myself. My plan so far was working beautifully.

In case you don't know the rules of dodge ball or maybe you played by a different set of rules than we did, here are the basics. Two equally numbered teams get on either side of a line and throw the ball at the other players. If the ball hits you, you are out. If they catch a ball you throw, you are out. My plan was to get out as soon as possible. I did not want to be pummeled by the ball, I preferred to have the other team catch my throw, but I couldn't just wait around, for a chance to throw it either. I couldn't even been sure I would get an opportunity to throw it.

That day while we were playing, someone threw the ball at me, and I was the first one out. When this happened, I was lying on the gym floor, and I had an epiphany. I could not believe I had not thought of this before. When I got up, I began to limp toward the sideline, and said to Coach Reyner, "Coach, I believe I am injured, and there is no way I will be able to play anymore today. I will have to sit the rest of the day out. I am sorry for overexerting myself and letting my team down, but most of all I'm sorry for letting you down." I was so surprised when he believed my display of remorse; I lost a little more respect for him. I went and sat with the rest of the burnouts until the end of class.
I was doing this every day. I was the absolute last person picked on any team. If the ball did not hit me, I would have to get it somehow, and it was not as easy as it sounds. Anytime I did get the ball, I could just lob it underhanded over the line to be sure someone would easily catch it. I

made no attempt to make it look good. I wanted to sit on my ass and do nothing, and I wanted the coach to know this is what I was doing. I had no ambition of being a professional athlete or Coach Reyner's student-who-overcame-adversity success story for him to try and sell as an after-school special.

As soon as the ball hit me, I would just fake an injury. If I became tired of waiting for the ball to hit me, I would settle for it coming close. I would say it hit me. My own team would scream in protest and argue, but I would say, "No, no, no, I want to be fair. It tipped me." The burnouts would be rolling with laughter, and this became my new motivation. I was having more fun screwing up everyone else's time than I did sitting on my ass doing nothing.

When I got to gym class, I remember the burnouts rooting for me yelling, "Yahhhh Nardone, whooooooo!" They were genuinely looking forward to watching me screw up the game. It really felt great to have fans. They also cheered when I came out of the dressing room and when the game began. One of them even made a little poster and held it up while I was on the floor.

When I got back to the bleachers, we would review what I had done and even discuss new and innovative ways to screw tomorrow's game up as well. Gym class was now what I most looked forward to at school every day. Those grungy looking people in the bleachers were far more than burnouts to me. They had all become something I never thought I would have. They were fans of Tom Nardone. They were also my friends. They looked forward to seeing what I would do next.

Coach Reyner eventually caught on. He pulled me to a side one day and said, "Okay, Nardone. I should have known better than to believe that bullshit you fed me about growing and self-discovery. If you want to sit on your ass and be a waste case for the rest of your life then go right ahead. You will pass my class if you will just sit down and not disrupt the game and celebrate your contempt for everybody who is making an effort."

Of course what I heard him say was, "Hey, Tom, you won, and I lost."

While this brief period of fame and victory was fun, it was also short-lived. Soon enough it was back to the usual bullshit I was beginning to grow accustomed to. Most of my grades were good by now, but I still had a big problem.

I was passing Mrs. Borden's class, but barely hanging on by a thread. Things had not gotten any better with her, and I was sure she did not like me. My cheating partner and I had gotten my grade to a strong D, but we had a big project we had to present at the end of the year. We had to pick a country and do a report on it. We also had to work in groups of four. Mrs. Borden let the class pick our own groups. I was in the nerd group that formed as a result of them being different. We were the last four, and we came together simply by default. My group picked Sweden. One of the guys had a watch from Sweden, so for this reason they picked Sweden.

My group labeled me as a dumb ass from the beginning, so our weekly "work as a team" project was actually all of them talking about what they will be doing, and me, sitting there getting a jump on my homework, so that I could spend more time sitting on my ass, relaxing and watching TV when I got home. I really did try to be a part of the group. Every time I opened my mouth, they would tell me not to be stupid, or they would ask me if I was a retard; therefore, I just sat quietly and let them have their fun.

I thought since they did not really have any friends either, maybe this would be a good chance for me to make some friends. It did not happen. They had the same problems I did with the other students. This was the only chance they would ever have to be in a position of power, and they decided to exclude me from being a real part of the group.

They worked on this every Friday for twelve weeks, and we were all to give a presentation, not only to the class, but also to the parents. I could not believe that Mrs. Borden had to invite the parents. She was adamant about the invitations. She even made an assignment out of the damn invitation form. We had to have our parents sign it and indicate if they were going to attend or not. This would count as a test grade. She was clear, "You can do it and get a one hundred or you can not do it and get a zero." I forged mine, and she didn't notice, but I got a real nice test grade for it.

Mrs. Borden, during the last two weeks of our preparation, reminded us that this would be a group effort on a group project, and we would get a grade as a group. Everyone in the group would be getting the same grade. I could not believe my luck. I was going to ride in on the coattails of the same group of assholes who had given me nothing but shit for twelve weeks. I could not have been more pleased.
At our last meeting, one of the others said to me, "Tommy, what are you going to bring in for a project?"

I said, "I'm not bringing anything."

He answered back speaking on behalf of the group, "You can't bring nothing. You will hurt all of our grades!"

I answered him back very politely and said, "Look, I don't give a shit. I tried to be a part of the group, and you guys wanted to be a bunch of assholes. Now, you realize that my lack of involvement is going to hurt you, and you want my input? You asked me what I am bringing, and I said nothing."

He said, "Well could you at least just bring in a Swedish food?"

I said, "Fine." I had every intention of having my mom whip up some meatballs or some other food. I did not even know what in the hell they ate in Sweden. I hoped my mom would know.

I went home for the weekend, and I did not even give a single thought to this project until it was too late. I forgot all about the Swedish food. I remembered it Sunday night after my mom and Dad had already gone to bed. I had no project. I was going to show up with nothing, and I had no idea what I was supposed to do or say when it came time for me to speak. I could not avoid having speak to a large group of strangers the next day, so I could not show up empty-handed. If I had nothing to present, then Mrs. Borden would be able to justify giving me a zero.

I got on my bike around midnight, rode up to the grocery store and bought a Big Block candy bar. That would be my project. I heard one of the group members saying they made chocolate in Sweden. I did not know if my big block was made in Sweden, but I had no problem lying to a bunch of strangers about it under the circumstances.

The next day at school, we were giving our presentations. There were six groups. The second group was finishing, and we were next. I saw in each of the two groups who presented before us, the person who brought food had prepared very elaborate entrees. I could not believe how nice they looked. They were serving portions to the guests after their presentation was over. Serving the food seemed to be a big part of the presentations, but I did not know this was required at the end of our presentation. I thought, *There are thirty people out there. How in the hell am I going to divide a candy bar up into thirty pieces?*

It was time for our group to present. While all of the groups were impressive, our group was miles ahead of them. The first person in our group had a beautiful three dimensional map with Sweden's topography. This map, showed the elevation of the country. He included weather conditions and trends and a lot of geological information about the landscape of the Sweden.

Our next person outlined the entire history of Sweden and included the hierarchy of their current government and their financial position in the world market. He even dressed as one Sweden's historical figures. I

94

actually found his presentation somewhat boring, but it was nevertheless incredible.

The girl in our group was dancer, so she outlined the culture of Sweden. She brought in music and wore an authentic dress she made herself and performed a dance which was a custom of some kind in Sweden. She actually got a standing ovation for her performance. I really felt she earned it. Then, it was my turn.

Now, bear in mind, I was following the dancer girl, who just received the only standing ovation for the entire two hours it took to get through all the presentations. I was a fifteen-year-old kid in the eighth grade, and I went out there in front of thirty complete strangers and began my first attempt ever at public speaking. I also missed Mrs. Borden's instructions where she explained we were to dress up for this. I was the only boy in my class without a button up shirt and a tie.

In a room full of nicely dressed parents, teachers and students, I walked out in front of all of them wearing sweat pants, a dirty T-shirt with a spaghetti stain on it and a torn pair of sneakers with no socks. I stood in front of over sixty people, and said, "Hello, my name is Tom Nardone. In Sweden, they make and eat a lot of chocolate, so I brought a Big Block candy bar. *(very long pause)* Are there any questions?"

There were no questions.

There was however, an abundance of silence. It was the exact scenario, for which people use the idiom of "crickets". I stood up there looking out to a sea of confused and disappointed faces. They looked around the room and avoided eye contact with me. This was the level of embarrassment they felt for me. When I noticed Mrs. Borden, she was in the back of the room with her back to the wall, and her head down staring at the floor. When I asked if there were any questions, she slowly and shamefully put her face down into her hands.

The silence was broken by the lone clap of one sympathetic parent. Slowly the others joined in and participated in this half-assed applause of which I did not even deserve. When the clapping began, Mrs. Borden quickly raised her head back up and her disposition had changed from embarrassment to happiness, but then to fury the minute she made eye contact with me.

Mrs. Borden could not get to me fast enough. She pulled me aside and took me away from the others. I never saw a woman get so angry. She was outraged at what she perceived to be a mockery of her assignment. She got me out into the hall way alone and asked me all kinds of questions: "Was that your best effort?", "Why didn't you say more than two sentences?" and "Were you trying to embarrass me?" She asked me to answer her.

My response was, "Mrs. Borden, what do you want me to do with this chocolate bar?" Her eyes got so big, and she almost laughed, but went quickly back to being angry.

She then said, "I swear if I wasn't a teacher I would give you a real good answer for that question, now get out of my sight!"

I walked back to rejoin my group. They were devastated, and I just didn't give a shit. I just stood against the wall with my group, and the other students who had completed their presentations. I stood there and watched the rest of this foolishness, as I enjoyed the entire Big Block candy bar, which I was denied the opportunity to share.

Mrs. Borden spoke to me the following day. She explained to me it killed her to have to award my group an A+ given my own lack of effort. She felt my classmates worked very hard, and she thought it would be unfair to punish them for what she described as "my own selfish lack of concern for the group". She sarcastically ended our conversation by saying, "Congratulations on your A, Mr. Nardone."

To which I replied, "Thank you." Tom

Nardone Wins!

Looking back, I don't feel bad about any of this. I laugh when I think about getting an A+ for bringing in a Big Block candy bar and eating it without even having to share. This was a group project, and I was excluded from the group until they realized their own grade might be affected. I looked at all of these people as some sort of a secret society. A society of which I was not a part. I honestly believe if they had included me in their little group of nerds, I would have been far more engaged in the discussions and would have put forth an effort in the project. Two weeks later school ended. That was it. Eighth grade was over. Middle school was over.

I did not get what I deserved, but I did get what I expected from middle school. Aside from Mrs. Chambers, and the Tom Nardone fan club in gym class, I had no good memories from middle school. I always felt I was by myself. I had only a few people whom I spoke to while I was there, and I dreaded every day I walked through the front door after getting off the bus each morning.

I never had to go back. Mrs. Tempest, Mrs. Durfee, Mrs. Borden, Coach Reyner and all the other assholes would never see or hear from me again. I can't even tell you how freeing this felt.

I did not have high hopes for high school. I had no reason to think things would be any better. This would be a new school with new people, and I was just hopeful it would go quickly.

Chapter 8

Ninth grade was the first year I just didn't believe things would be any different. I always managed to maintain a positive attitude before every school year, but I had been conditioned from experience things were not going to change for me. This year I had no hopes or aspirations of being accepted. I had no belief that I might have an easy go of it. I was sure I would have problems with my teachers and other students. I did not even plan to have any friends. All I wanted to do was go to school, be invisible and try to do my work well enough to pass my classes, not anger my teachers and prevent my parents from being disappointed.

I did manage to keep my grades up, but aside from grades, ninth grade was just a repeat of every other year I spent in school. I got through it, and I passed. I actually remember the ninth grade least of all.

By this time, I just quit caring. So many people told me I was stupid, retarded, a waste, a geek, a moron or a loser so many times I guess I was starting to believe it. The only thing that helped me all through the years of school were the friends I had in the neighborhood: Brad, Paul, Matt and of course, Brody Bricker. I don't know what I would have done without those guys. They were my only friends.

The summer between the ninth and tenth grade would be a defining one. This was summer when I embraced music. I was home and flipping through the channels. I decided to watch this local show that played heavy metal videos. Donald watched this all the time. The last video they played was for a song called "The Last in Line" by Dio. I will never forget it. I immediately got on my bike and rode up to the record store and bought all the albums by Dio. This was the first time I fell in love.

I loved the eighties' metal genre. I not only embraced the music, but the lifestyle and the attitude. This had a profound effect on the rest of my life. I quit caring about everybody at school. I did not care about having friends. I was not thinking about my future and having a good job. I slowly and systematically began to care less and less about many things in my life. I discovered through the act of not caring, things I used to worry about no longer mattered. I kept my grades up and did the things around the house I was supposed to do, but nothing else. I had already stopped caring, but the difference was I now chose not to care.

College was the last thing on my mind. I could see what type of people were talking about going to college, and I did not want to follow them.

I hated and despised all of these people. Why would I want to do what they were doing? I saw no need to wrack my brain in college with these assholes. I decided the only reason I was in high school was to finish it and get out. If I made friends along the way, so be it, but it did not matter anymore. I had plenty of friends in the box I used to store my cassette tapes. Maiden, Priest, Metallica and the Crüe were the only friends I needed, and they never once let me down.

It was the first day of my tenth grade year in high school. For the past ten years, the first day of school was a very difficult and frustrating day for me. I would get nervous and worry about making friends. I worried whether or not people were going to have a problem with me, and I would try like hell not to do anything to give them cause to make fun of me. I would wake up, take a shower, stare at the mirror and try to conceal my acne. I would wear my best clothes and comb my hair. I would go to great lengths to try to look my very best, but it had gotten me nowhere. This is how it went every morning before I went to school, and especially the first day, but never again.

On that morning, I decided I would do things a little different. This day was not going to be as any other first day of school I ever had. I woke up, rolled out of bed and put on a pair of pants and a T-shirt. I went downstairs and put on my shoes. I did not see the need to take a shower; I did not see the need to brush my teeth; I did not see the need to put on my acne medication or even to give a shit about my appearance. I did not even so much as look at a mirror. I did put on my deodorant because I didn't want to smell my own underarms. On this day, I was happy. On this day, I was free, and on this day, for the first time in my life, I went to school as Tom Nardone.

I just completely quit caring about what anyone saw in me, and I quit caring about what they believed me to be. Nothing anyone ever said or did would ever change the direction of my life. I did not like who those people were, and I did not want my name associated with these kinds of people. They could all go straight to hell, as far as I was concerned. Socially speaking, I completely shut down and decided I would no longer participate. I was secure about being the person I was, and I did not want to be anyone else.

There were people who tried to give me a hard time, but it had no effect on me. I usually did not even look in their direction. I ignored them, or I was just so disinterested I did not even hear them. Sometimes if their remarks had any comedic value, I would even laugh. I discovered trying to please everyone and being rejected was no different to me than failing. Before, I made an effort to fit in, and this effort was found by the

99

masses to be unacceptable. Things were different now as I made no effort. You can't fail if you don't even try, and you can't be rejected if you don't attempt to be a part of a person's life or a group.

I was making friends, and the friends I made did not have any interest in knowing those people any more than I did. I looked at these people as the good guys. The people I became friends with were also headbangers and burnouts, but they were nice and interesting to me. They never judged me or mocked me or gave a damn what I wore or what I did. I was the only one of these people who did not smoke pot, and other than mentioning it here and there, they never pressured me to do so. They had no need for me to act a certain way. I could just be who I was.

My grades were up, and I could not have been happier. I found happiness when I decided I was okay to just be who I was, and I wanted to help other people. I was not necessarily proactive as if I were on some sort of crusade, but when I saw somebody being harassed by other people in the class, I got involved. I would make it a point to get to know this person, and find out who they were. I would just start talking to them, and pretty soon we were friends and got along great. I might loan them a cassette tape of the bands I listened to, and then before too long, they quit giving a damn and came to school dressed as the rest of the like-minded headbanger people. I never suggested or encouraged this. It was just the natural course of things. They also, for the first time in their lives, came to school happy, just as I did.

Another thing happened when I stopped giving a damn about what others thought of me. I was able to focus on other things, such as my schoolwork. I still had many problems in school academically, but I was able to keep my grades up. My grades would never again be a problem for me. I was able to focus on my work, and the only classes I failed were the ones I knew I did not need in order to graduate. I failed a few classes intentionally. I had the mindset of a proud underachiever.

In psychology class, I only had a slight interest. I would listen to the class discussions because I found them interesting. When it came time to do the work, I put my head on my desk and went to sleep. I didn't feel too bad since the teacher did not seem to mind. She never said a word about it.

As for the grades I felt mattered, I was on top of them, and I had a lot of free time on my hands after school. I used this "free time" to watch lots of television and listen to music. I would spend most days lying around the house doing nothing. My dad was not very impressed with this. I was sixteen years old and did not even want a driver's license.

My dad came home from work one day and saw me lying on the couch and said, "You know, Tommy, you turned sixteen a month ago. Maybe since you have all this free time, you should try to see if you can get a job before summer gets here."

I asked, "Dad, do you want me to get a job for the summer?" I really loved his answer.

He said, "Tommy, it isn't that I need you to get a job. It's that I don't want to have to come home from work every day this summer, and see your lazy ass lounging around on my furniture."

I took this to mean dad would like to see me get a job, and even at the age of sixteen, I still needed my dad to be pleased with me. Apparently, it was no longer enough my grades were on track. My dad had expectations of me to grow up and be a man. I was not against the idea of having a job. The idea of it had not really occurred to me.

I got to school the next day, and I told a friend of mine named Travis I had to get a job. He told me he was a shift leader at a fast food restaurant and if I went down there after school, he would hire me the same day. I was pretty excited about having a job. I couldn't wait to see the look on my dad's face when I told him I got a job the first day I looked.

I went to see Travis after school, and true to his word, he hired me immediately just as he promised he would. He even said I could start that night. He did the paperwork, and got me a uniform. I was now employed at my first job. I could not believe it. I met some of the other people on the night crew I would be working with, and I thought this was amazing. The only people Travis would ever hire were burnouts and headbangers. When I got there, I was happy to find I knew the people I would be working with from school. Travis told me when people from school who gave us a hard time came in to try to get a job, he just laughed at them and told them to get the hell out of his restaurant.

I called the house and told mom I was working and would not be home until 11 p.m. I also asked her to let my dad know. My mom was caught off guard by my call. She said it was fine and was quite surprised since she was not privy to the conversation I had with my father the day before. Dad walked in the door, looked at the couch and noticed that my ass wasn't spread out across it. He asked my mom, "Where is the lump?"

Mom said, "Tommy got a job, and he won't be home until 11 p.m."

My dad couldn't believe it. He actually got right back in his car, told my mom he was going to get dinner, drove to the restaurant where I was working and went to the drive-thru window. Dad did not want to come in and embarrass me so he got in line at the window and placed his order. When he got to the window, he paid for his order, and asked if a new person named Tommy was working. Travis came over to me and told me somebody was at the drive-thru for me. I went there, and it was my dad. He just started laughing. He could not stop laughing, but he managed to gain his composure long enough to congratulate me and tell me he would see me at the house later.

When I got home at 11:30, my dad was sitting on the couch waiting for me. Dad stayed up late to talk to me when I got home. He was more excited than I was. He had many questions for me. We talked a while, and then he told me I should get some rest. He said, "Tommy, I sure am proud of you son." It had been quite a while since I gave him a reason to be proud of me. I guess bad grades and watching television were not the best way to impress my father. Work, however, was a great way to impress my father. Upon getting this job, he became a powerful ally which I would need very soon, as my mother would find herself very unhappy about my new-found job.

This job quickly became very important to me for a few reasons. My father's excitement about my being in the "working world" was very important. I would be making money, and I could now buy as many albums as I wanted, but the biggest reason was actually due to something it would prevent me from being able to do.

The first week I was working, I was scheduled to work on from 10 a.m. until 7 p.m. on Sunday. My mom woke me and my brothers up Sunday morning and told us it was time to get ready for church. When I woke I realized I had to be to work at 10 a.m., so there was no way I could go to church. I was ecstatic about this. Having this job just got better and better. Then, I realized there was a problem. I did not even think about my mother and how she might feel. I took no pleasure in disappointing her, but I did not want to quit my job.

I was not sure who to mention this to first. I figured I would tell my mom first. I thought maybe she would be understanding and allow me to continue working. I could not have been more wrong. I went to my mom, and carefully explained to her I had to go to work, and consequently I would not be able to attend church with her and my two brothers. My mother's response was heated when she said, "Oh, Hell no! You will just have to quit that damn job because you are going to church with us!" She was very angry, and I decided I couldn't win this argument with her. I knew my father was my only ally in this, so I would have to appeal to him.

When my mom finished, I went downstairs to explain to my dad I was going to have to quit my job. Dad said, "What?"

I said, "Easy, Dad. Mom says I have to go to church, and they said they can't let me off every Sunday."

My dad got up out of his easy chair, pointed at me and said, "Wait!" He flew up the stairs, and he and my mother went to battle stations. I heard all kinds of yelling and arguing. It was not pleasant to hear. They were at it for a while, but my father emerged as the victor. He came back and said, "You are not to quit your job!" I just said okay and went back to bed. I went to work that day and told my boss I wanted to work every Sunday for the rest of my career at that restaurant, from 10 a.m. to 7 p.m. So it was written, and so it was done.

My mother would calm down and eventually she just accepted it, but Donald was not happy at all about this. He was furious. He couldn't believe he had to go to church every Sunday and I didn't. One Sunday morning weeks later, I got up before my mother or my brothers. I did not have to be in until twelve, so I went downstairs to watch TV with my father. I knew my mother would be waking Donald and Phillip up, and they would have to get ready for church. I wanted Donald to see me hanging out with dad as he walked out the door to go to church. Mom woke them, and they began to get ready. Donald had an awful look on his face as he came downstairs wearing his Sunday clothes. He would not look at me because he was too mad.

When it was time to go, Mom, Donald and Phillip, left the house. A few minutes later, Donald came running back in because he forgot his Sunday school book. When he went upstairs, I got up, went to the door and waited for him to return, so I could speak to him at the door before he left. When he came back, I stopped him and said, "Hey, Donald, listen. I know you are mad, but listen. Today, while you are at church, I want you to listen to the service and really try to get something from it." You could have fried an egg on his face as he went out the door. My dad overheard this and told me if I ever did that again, he would make me quit my job.

This is all basically how my life went for the duration of my time in school. I worked my job and went to school for the remainder of my high school career without incident. I passed my exams for my senior year of high school. I decided not go to the graduation ceremony. I did not want to have to go back to that school ever again. I was thrilled it was over. I told my mom not to worry about the graduation ceremony because I was not planning on attending it. My mom said, "The hell you aren't."

My father seldom ever wanted to leave the house, but he made an exception for this momentous occasion. My parents attended my graduation ceremony, and I was officially finished with school. I had managed to get through all thirteen years to get that magical, coveted piece of paper. My parents were both proud, as was I. When we got home my mother said congratulations and hugged me. She was so proud. My father put his arm around me, and said something to me, I will not ever forget. "Tommy, when everyone was going up there to get their diplomas, I noticed they all stood up straight and walked very nice and proud, but when you went up there, you just walked like you always do. I thought that was great, son."

I imagine the way I felt when I graduated was much the same as a prisoner feels the day he is released. In every way, school for me was as a prison. I had no plans of ever being in school again.

I was a different person entirely as a result of my experiences at school. I went into the public school system as a meek, quiet, shy and curious child. I wanted to make friends and have fun in this new place. I was full of hope, and I wanted to do very well at everything I attempted. I was, however, all but denied this, and I became bitter, jaded and indifferent.

I never made peace until I was introduced to it by my newest, closest friend: indifference. By the time I graduated from high school, I had an indifference to the whole world. I did not care about anything outside of my own interests. I did not want to meet people. I did not want to go to social gatherings. I thought almost everything was stupid. The majority of my life had been spent in a world which, for whatever reason, would not accept me. I tried every way I knew to fit into the crowd. The person I had become up to this point was not born, but made.

The majority or my experiences up to this point were of ridicule, failure, disappointment and finally indifference. I might have gone on to college. I might have taken a better path for my future, but my own experiences taught me I could not possibly be happy this way. I had no reason to believe caring about anything was going to change anything. For me, life was not about doing things to make things better and feeling good about myself. For me, life was about avoiding things and not feeling bad about myself. This is what school taught me. I have no regrets, but sometimes I wonder how things had turned out if I were not excluded by my peers.

I learned I did not need those people. Indifference had become my new best friend. Indifference shadowed me from the clutches of hope and optimism, thereby ending my ridicule and depression. It was only in the presence of my indifference my grades improved. It was only in the presence of indifference I found my job and graduated from high school. My friend, indifference taught me what I believed was the truth was about people and about the world. Indifference at this time was not an acquaintance; it was my soul mate, a true friend, who would never let me suffer. I could not ever imagine letting go it. How could I let go of the only friend who taught me to be happy?

Indifference had become my closest friend, and I feel it served its purpose. I did not believe it was the best way to live the rest of my life. This was how I felt upon graduating from high school. I now know the truth about my indifference toward the world. It was not nearly as bad-ass, tough, admirable or romantic as I thought it was. In truth, I see now the indifference I had was nothing more than a way for me to cope with my fear. The truth is I was frightened of everything I saw.

The next phase of my life offered the most indisputable proof of the fear inside me, and I lied to everybody about my reasons for doing it. The truth is I was just scared, and I just ran away. I did not know what any of the right answers were in my life. I just figured they were somewhere else.

Chapter 9

My joining the Navy was in large part my brother Donald's doing. A few months before I graduated, Donald and I were out driving around. Donald thought it would be fun to go talk to a Marine recruiter. I agreed, so we went in and sat down with him.

When we entered the Marine recruiting office, an enormous Marine welcomed us. We sat down, and he looked at us for about 15 seconds in silence before he asked us, "So, do you boys think you have what it takes to wear this uniform?"

Donald asked the enormous Marine, "Hey, man, can you smoke pot in the Marines?"

I watched this marine jump out of his chair, pick up the phone, and say, "Boy, I oughta throw this damn phone at you!"

Donald turned white and apologized. Things calmed down a bit as the staff sergeant continued. I was listening to him, and what he was saying made good sense to me, and I really did not have any plans for my post-graduation. I decided on the way home that I was going to join the United States Marine Corps.

When I got home, I couldn't wait to tell my dad. He did not like this at all. He suggested I talk to more people before making a quick decision. I agreed, and I went the next day to talk to with the Army. I was convinced right away. I told the army recruiter to sign me up right then. He was not expecting me to agree so soon, and he did not have the forms he needed. He was very excited about me joining.

He said, "Look, tomorrow is Saturday. Can you be here at seven in the morning?"

I said, "I will be here."

I was there the next day just before seven in the morning, but he was not. I waited and waited for fifteen or twenty minutes, but he still had not showed up. I told myself, "Screw this! I will have to come back on Monday," but on my way out, the Navy recruiter saw me and while sitting at his desk he said, "Hey, how are you?" So I just joined the Navy that day rather than come back for the Army guy.

Dad still could not believe I joined the Navy as a result of my impatience, but he was proud that I was making decisions for my future. I had saved up some money from my job and quit a month before I shipped out for the Navy. I spent the month before I left just seeing friends and hanging out. I was bored and was looking forward to the next chapter of my life.

It was July 4, 1990, early in the afternoon when the doorbell rang. My recruiter had arrived to take me to the airport. It was this moment, for the first time it occurred to me I was leaving my mom, dad and brothers. I began to cry as I thought about all the things we had gone through as a family. I was angry at Donald for his involvement in getting me thinking about the military. I know it was not his intention. I did not want to leave, but I had no choice at this point. It was hard leaving my family. I was leaving the protection of my parents who loved me and cared for me for so many years. Donald was not there because he was too upset and did not want to deal with the sadness.

The hardest thing about my leaving, and the thing I felt the worst about, was leaving behind my little brother, Phillip. He was not as emotional as I was, and this was the first time I ever saw him cry. Phillip was so quiet most of the time, and when I saw him, I couldn't believe I was leaving. He was my little brother, and I would no longer be there for him. I wouldn't be able to drive him to school, or help him when he needed me. I had always been a big brother to Phillip. I worried what he would do without me. He was young, and I did not know if he understood why I was leaving.

I hugged all of my family and tearfully walked out of my parents' house. I was not doing very well at all in the car, as we drove to the processing station in Atlanta. Within about fifteen minutes, I was just fine and back to being very excited about starting my new life. I really did not know what to expect, and I had high hopes of doing well and making my parents proud.

San Diego, California was my home during boot camp. It was very bad, and I hated every boring minute of it. I did not have any real problems because I was scared shitless of doing anything wrong; therefore, I was quite focused on what was required of me. There were literally, no distractions in boot camp because all there was in boot camp was boot camp. The thing I thought might present the biggest challenge was folding my clothes. The Navy apparently is pretty serious about this in boot camp.

Folding your clothes in boot camp was ridiculous. It was something they required us to do in a specific way in order to teach us to follow directions. All we ever heard was "Pay attention to detail!" We had some people who were almost finished with boot camp come in to show us how the Navy expected us to fold our clothes. The people who taught us were thorough, but I knew I would screw this up, so I came up with a scheme.

I had the instructors show me how to fold two complete sets of all the clothes I was required to keep in my locker. I left those two sets alone for the entire time I was in boot camp. When the laundry came in, I would get only one set of clothes out, and leave the rest to go back to the laundry even though they were not dirty. I sent my clothes that were actually dirty along with them. I never folded anything, but I aced every inspection we ever had because I was smart enough to figure out how to take the thinking process out of the equation. Near the end of boot-camp, it was time for me to be one of the ones to help the new recruits learn how to fold their clothes. I could be of no help at all to them since I had very little experience.

I thought it would never end; it was the longest two months in my entire life. When it did end, I went home on leave and saw my parents. I was so happy to see them. I wore my uniform home, and my dad picked me up at the airport. Everybody was fine; even Phillip was okay. It was so nice to see him.

After being back home for three weeks, I went back to San Diego for A-school. This was about nine months. From there I went to BESS (Basic Enlisted Submarine School) in Groton, Connecticut. When I finished submarine school, I checked in at my actual duty station at Pearl Harbor Naval Submarine Base in Hawaii, just over one year after having left home. I had been through so much training and school I just wanted to get to my submarine. I was so curious about it, and the people I would be working with.

When I checked in at Pearl Harbor, I was not in uniform as I was supposed to be. The guy at the desk did not even care. He just told me we needed to hurry up before someone saw me and asked questions. After he checked me in, he informed me my "boat", as they called it, had left one day before I arrived to go to sea and would not be back for six weeks. I asked him, "What am I supposed to do until then?" I could not believe his answer.

He said, "Do you like to surf?" I explained to him that I had never tried surfing, but I needed to know what I was supposed to do for the next few weeks. He said, "You can do whatever you want to do. Sleep, surf, drink, and go to the beach. You are in Hawaii, and your boat is not here. This is what we do in the Navy. We wait around, so enjoy yourself."

For the first six weeks, I was on vacation in Hawaii. I was not sure how there was nothing for me to do on the whole base. I saw people working at the barracks where I lived every day. It did not look like any fun, and I was happy the guy excluded me from it.

I explored all over the island to see what people saw in this place. Hawaii was the most beautiful state I had ever seen. I had a blast for the first six weeks I was there. It was a long six weeks, but it ended when my boat pulled into port.

I made sure I was on the pier to meet my submarine as it pulled into the harbor. It did not look any different than most of the boats that were there. I was very excited to meet the guys. I already knew I would be hazed being I was new, and it was just the nature of the submarine community.

The COB or Chief of the Boat met me on the pier and asked me, "Nardone, what have you been doing for the last six weeks?"

I told him the truth. I said, "Nothing, COB."

He said, "Son, I am not your friend asking you what you have been up to! I want to know where you have been working for the past six weeks."

I told him what the person at squadron who checked me in said, and he just rolled his eyes and said, "Why, am I not surprised?" He pointed and said, "Well, do you see that guy over there? He is going to be your boss. Go meet him, and he will tell you what you're going to be doing."

I felt as if I dodged a bullet because I figured I might be in some kind of trouble for my activities over the previous six weeks.

The man the COB pointed to was Andy Webber. I went to him and introduced myself. He was happy to meet me, and he introduced me to the rest of the people in the department. I met Rob Lim, who was a great guy, and I met the man who would be my "Sea Dad", Don Kwisinski, or as we called him, Ski. Ski's job was to help me and show me the ropes. I got the idea he did not want the job. We would later have a falling out, and Lim would take over where Ski left off. Webber explained to me I would be in Deck Division and our boat, which I was so anxious to go to sea with, would be going into dry-dock in a few days. I would have to wait even longer now before I went to sea.

Deck division was responsible for the exterior of the submarine. Specifically, we were the ones who did all of the grinding, chipping, painting and maintenance to make it look pretty. Aside from the people in my division, most of the people on the boat were not nice at all to me. It was nothing personal, but that is the way it is on a submarine when you are the new guy.

New people all have the same name. We are referred to as Nub. NUB is actually an acronym, and it stands for Non-Useful Body. I asked someone why we are called Nub, and the answer was, "Because all you do while we are at sea is drink the water, eat the food, breathe the air and fill the shit-tanks." It is only after I got certified to stand a watch I was afforded any respect by the majority of the crew. Until such time, I was just a Nub and was given all the shitty jobs no one else wanted to do themselves. I was okay with it.

I didn't go straight to deck division. They decided that I would be working in the galley on the dry-dock facility. We were there for a long time. I hated working in the galley. After I left the dry-dock each night, I went into the submarine to study and get a jump on my qualifications. I was interested and excited to learn about the submarine. This was every new person's primary responsibility until they are certified. After two months we finished our repairs, and put the boat back in the water. The COB took me out of the galley and put me in Deck Division.

Chief Laveen was my boss while I was in deck division. He was a short, stocky man from the Dominican Republic, and I really liked the way he talked. Having spent all my life in the southeastern United States, I had not spoken to many people with a foreign accent. He was always nice to me, and I really enjoyed having him as my chief.

The boat, having been out of dry-dock for a few days, was about to go to sea to conduct sea trials. We did this to make sure the boat was operational before we could be put on patrol. I had about three days in deck division, and Chief Laveen would give me my first big job on the night before sea trials.

Chief Laveen said to me, "Oh! Nardone! I have a really big job for you tonight. I don't think you are going to get any sleep. You see that sail?" The sail is the big, tall teardrop shaped part of the submarine's exterior.

I said, "Yes, Chief."

He said, "Those clowns you work with did not finish painting. That is why the sail is green. That is a primer. You understand, Nardone?"

I said, "Yes, Chief."

Chief Laveen smiled and said, "OK, good good. Now, there is black paint over there on the pier, do you see it?"

"Yes, Chief."

Chief Laveen said, "Good good, Nardone. You need to take that paint and paint the entire sail. Don't miss any spots. The paint covers good so

110

just go over it once, and you should be OK. The captain himself told me to take care of this, and I am taking a risk by having you do this for me. Do you understand what I need, Nardone? Do you have any questions for me?"

"No, Chief."

"Good, Nardone. That is real good. I will see you in the morning, Nardone. I know you will do a real good job for me."

As he walked down the pier, I said "Good night, Chief." He waved his hand in the air without looking back.

I cannot imagine what in the hell was he thinking. It is a shame he didn't get a chance to work with me a little bit before deciding I was the man for this job. There was nobody else in deck division on the boat that night. If I ran into a snag, there was no one to ask for help. I had never painted anything in my life before. It really is a shame that he didn't need me to pull weeds because I knew how to do that pretty well. I would just have to learn how to paint while I was doing it. I just had to hope it would not end in disaster.

It was thirteen hours until the chief would be back. I went down and ate dinner. I went back up topside and looked at the sail. I thought it would be easy enough. The sail was green so I just had to make it black again. I went to the pier, got my roller and put it on the end of the stick just as I saw them doing earlier that day. I opened a new bucket of paint. It was black as it could be. I went to the boat and poured the paint into my tray. I put the roller into the paint and began painting the sail. It was going great. I could not believe how well it was going. I thought I was finished, and I remembered I had to do the top of the sail as well.

This was the first time I ever went all the way up to the top of the sail where the bridge was. I was having a great time. I used a brush to paint the bridge. The bridge is where the Captain goes as the boat is heading out to sea so I wanted to be sure, I did a good job. After only about six hours, I was finished with the whole thing. I put all my stuff back on the pier, and got everything cleaned up. I was tired so I went to bed. I couldn't even sleep because I was so excited about going to sea. I could not wait to see the look on the chief's face when he saw what a good job I had done painting the sail.

Later that morning, we were only a couple of hours away from my first time at sea with my submarine. Everybody would see the sail I painted, and I found myself looking it over the next morning before the chief arrived. I could not find anything I had missed. I stood on the pier and waited for Chief Laveen to come in. I saw him walking toward the boat.

He came to the brow, the bridge that you walk across to get to the boat from the pier, and I said, "Good morning, Chief."

He said, "Yeah, yeah, yeah." He then walked across the brow and went down the hatch without another word. I could not believe it. He did not say a word about the sail. What the hell is this? I wondered. Apparently, Chief Laveen just went down to get a cup of coffee. When he came back up, he was all about the sail.

I watched him walk all the way around it twice as he nodded his head continually. Nodding his head was a good sign. He stopped walking and looked at me and said, "Nardone, come over here and talk with me, buddy."

I ran across the brow and said, "What is the problem, Chief? I will fix it right now."

Chief Laveen laughed as he said, "No no, Nardone, you did a good job. Did you go in the bridge and paint?"

I proudly said, "Yes, I did Chief."

He laughed, "Oh, that is great, Nardone. This looks nice. You did a wonderful job. I am very proud of you." I could not have been happier. I was worried I would be the reason our boat could not go to sea, and I would let everyone down. I was thrilled my chief was proud of me. Other people as they got to the boat, asked me if I painted the sail, and I told them I did. I got some nods and some accolades from them. I was feeling great. I did a great job, at least it seemed I had.

When the boat started moving away from the pier, I was very excited. I got to stand on top of the boat and wave goodbye to all the family members. I did not know any of them, but I waved anyway. The boat began to go faster and faster, and the wind was blowing strong. It was a beautiful and warm day in Pearl Harbor. It was an amazing experience, listening to the sound my submarine made, as it barreled through the water. I had a slight fear of it all, but it was counteracted by my excitement.

The captain gave word for all of us to get below. We all went down the hatch. Seeing the crew go into at-sea-mode was amazing. It was an incredible transformation to see all of the people who were usually a bunch of pricks to me, transform into machines executing their jobs flawlessly to get our boat to sea. I was asked to go to the bridge and get the bridge box down before we dived the boat. The bridge box is a removable instrument and communications panel the officer looks at so he can talk to people who aren't in the bridge.

I went up this fifteen foot ladder and when I got to the top, it was beautiful. There were dolphins jumping high up into the air as our boat headed toward the dive point. I was watching all of this, and the Captain himself tapped me on the shoulder and laughed as he said, "Hey, Nardone, let me know when you are finished looking around, so I can dive my boat." This is how a nice captain politely says get the bridge box and get out of here with it. Moments later, we vanished under the surface of the Pacific Ocean.

Two days into what we called sea trials, we were told the admiral of the Pacific Submarine Fleet was going to board the boat and finish the sea trials with us. The whole ship began scrambling around to try to get the boat into shape. We spent the whole day cleaning, preparing and many other things in an attempt to make sure we were able to kiss his ass properly. When his transport boat was spotted through the periscope, the announcement was made over the PA, "Prepare to surface!"

When the boat surfaced, the officer of the deck and the lookout went up to the bridge. When they got up to the bridge, the officer of the deck started yelling at the top of his lungs, "Chief Laveen! Get your ass up here ASAP!" Chief Laveen went to the bridge and got his ass ripped. The sail I painted was green again, but there were wet patches of paint everywhere. The black wet paint got all over the Captains only set of dress whites he brought. When the Admiral boarded the boat it of course got all over his dress whites. The Admiral actually had a very unexpected, yet welcomed sense of humor about the whole incident. Chief Laveen, however, did not.

When Chief Laveen came down from the bridge, he asked one question, and he asked it with a level of fury I had not ever seen since in a human being. He asked, "Where is Nardone?!"

I was four feet from him, so I said, "I'm right here, Chief." He grabbed my arm and escorted me to the crew's sleeping quarters and chewed my ass in a way I have never heard of an ass being chewed. I thought my dad had skills, but Chief Laveen was king. I cannot even remember much of what he said. Seeing his anger overwhelmed me, and I could not believe how furious this sweet Dominican man had become. He was as a gentle teddy bear earlier that day, now he was pure evil. I have never seen a human being exhibit this range of demeanor. I was beside myself that I had let him down and scared at what the consequences would be for such a thing.

Apparently, the paint for a submarine is a rubber-based epoxy. This means that you have to mix part A with part B, and then paint. I just opened a can, and it was black. I thought it was submarine paint. Chief

Laveen saw how upset I was becoming at his anger, and he calmed down. I explained what I did, then he asked, "Nardone, where did you mix the paint?"

I said to him, "What do you mean mix the paint?"

He said, "Okay, Nardone, I am so sorry. This is not your fault. This is my fault. I thought you knew, but you had not painted the submarine before. I should have shown you the paint on the pier, and I should have shown you how to mix it. I was in a hurry to go home to my wife. You are fine, Nardone. Do not worry about this, please. I like you, Nardone, and I am sorry. I will fix this."

Chief Laveen took the hit for me. I was not in the least bit surprised this ended in a disaster. Even though it was not my fault, I felt I let my chief down. I still thought he would never trust me again. Chief Laveen was true to his word. When the crew started giving me a hard time about the sail debacle, he jumped right in and told them all to shut up because it was not my fault. When we got back, I asked him if I could be the one to paint the sail again, and he said sure. I mixed the paint properly, and the sail looked great.

I made my share of blunders while in the Navy. It did not happen often and never on as big a scale as the sail tragedy. I finished my qualifications in very short order and learned most of what I needed to know in order to do my job. I went to the interior communications division and did very well.

My ADHD was a source of trouble, but I was interested in the jobs I had on the boat; therefore, I usually did them very well. Some people were not looked at as being very bright, but I somehow managed to convince most of the crew my knowledge level was a little higher than average. I forgot things and looked stupid from time to time, but it was somehow masked by my ability to do my job well. There was only one person I was never able to win over. My XO. It is quite common for ADHD people to blurt things out which are inappropriate or to be misunderstood by others, and I suspect this is what the XO's trouble with me had stemmed from. I know he did not like me, and I never cared enough to inquire as to why.

The XO or Executive Officer, second only to the Captain, did not like me one bit. I never knew why. He once accused me of being a smart ass and claimed I was disrespectful to him. Chief Brighton was my chief, and he convinced the XO he would take care of it. Chief Brighton knew it was bullshit, and he told me not to worry about it. He told me to just go to the XO and apologize and it would solve the problem. I went to the XO and put on a show for his benefit. Without a look in my direction, he accepted my apology as if he didn't even have time to sit there on his fat ass and listen to me. I hoped this would be the end of it.

About two days after my apology, we were going to sea, and he was training a new officer how to be the OOD, officer of the deck. This XO was an incredible asshole to the new officers who came to the boat. They had not been trained and didn't know how to do anything. This was the place he most enjoyed displaying his arrogance. It was easy to impress someone who has never been on a submarine before. He loved busting the new officer's balls on their very first time at sea. This is just who he was, an asshole.

Part of my job on the boat was to do maintenance on all the open and shut indicators for the various valves and equipment on the submarine. One of which was for the "Head Valve". Before the ship can dive safely, the head valve must be shut.

The XO switched the periscope to video mode and turned it so that he could see the head valve on the video monitor in the control room. He then ordered the Chief of the Watch to shut the head valve. The Chief of the Watch threw the switch and said, "Head valve indicates shut."

The XO looked at the monitor and said, "Head valve is shut, diving officer, dive the shi…"

I interrupted his order and said, "XO, the head valve is not shut."

He looked at me with fire in his eyes and said, "Excuse me, Petty Officer Nardone. You interrupt the XO of a submarine when he is giving an order to dive the ship?"

I said, "Only if he orders it to dive with the head valve open, sir."

The XO ignited and shouted at the top of his lungs, "Petty Officer Nardone, I have been driving submarines for thirteen years, and you are going to tell me how…"

The captain hearing the XO shouting entered the control room and interrupted him. He knew me to be an above average technician. He told the XO to calm down and said with a slight chuckle, "Nardone, what is going on here and why are you questioning my XO and getting him so excited?"

I said, "Respectfully sir, the XO was trying to dive your boat with the head valve open. I don't think he wanted to do this, so I brought it to his attention. I don't exactly know what all the yelling was about, sir."

The XO said to the captain, "Sir, I am following the procedure. I watched the scope, and the head valve is shut."

I said, "Captain, no, it isn't. The head valve is open. The XO is mistaken."

The XO fired back yelling at me. The captain shouted, "Shut up! All of you!" The captain ordered the messenger of the watch to ask Chief Kroner to come to the control room. The Captain told the XO to set the periscope to video and bring the head valve up on the monitor.

While the messenger was getting the Chief, the Captain looked at me, smiled, leaned over and whispered in my ear, "Sure hope you are right about this one, Nardone."

I leaned to him and said to him, "Sir, do you think I would let it go this far if I was not?" He laughed gently and shook his head.

Chief Kroner entered the control room, and the Captain said, "Ahh, Chief Kroner, I need you to settle a dispute between Petty Officer Nardone and the XO."

Chief Kroner looked at me as if I was stupid. The Captain pointed to the monitor and said, "Chief Kroner, you see that?"

He said, "Yes, sir, I do. It's the head valve."

The Captain asked, "Tell me, Chief, what is the status of that head valve?"

Chief Kroner said immediately, "It is open sir."

The Captain thanked the chief and asked me what I thought was the problem was. I told him someone probably left the block of wood up there when they were doing the maintenance on it. I suggested the XO should send someone up there to pull it out, and it would shut just fine. The captain looked at the XO, and the XO ordered the messenger to the bridge. He came back down with a wet block of wood. This allowed the head valve to shut.

The XO quietly concurred that the head valve was now shut. The Captain whispered in my ear, "Well, Nardone, live to fight another day,

I suppose." He looked at the XO, but did not whisper when he said, "XO, come see me in my stateroom as soon as you can get yourself relieved!"

The XO glared at me, and I left the control room. The captain made the XO apologize to me. Later that day, Chief Kroner saw me in the passageway and said, "Nardone, you, my friend, have balls of steel. Nice work. You did the right thing standing up to that asshole." He shook my hand and went on his way.

My time in the Navy was not full of problems. My constant fear and my interest in the jobs I was assigned kept my attention level high. I did make plenty of mistakes here and there, and many of them were my fault. This was usually the exception, though, and not the rule. I managed to get through my four years, and I got through them well.

Looking back, I believe my time in the Navy was a success. I did very well, and I was recognized for many things I did. I believe I could have made a career of it, but I did not like the idea of going to sea for such a large portion of my life. Even though I was interested in this job, I could see myself being bored doing the same thing for another 16 years. I did not like the Navy as I once did, and I was counting the days until I got out. The other reason I wanted out was because I had not screwed it up yet. I wanted to leave this chapter of my life behind me and depart with a check in the win column. I was curious what I would be able to do in the real world with the things I had learned. I also missed my family.

After four consecutive years of success, I was sure I had things together, and I would have no problem back in the private sector. I was sure when I got out of the Navy, people would be so impressed when they learned of my service on a United States Naval submarine, and I would be hired instantly. I had no doubt I would just be able to pick my job from a list of many people who wanted me to work for their company. I could not have been more wrong.

Chapter 10

When I got out of the Navy, I decided to live in Greenville, South Carolina. I did not want to go back to the same town I left. I wanted a change of scenery. It was not far from my family, and there were plenty of jobs. In spite of all my efforts, I could not find a job in electronics or even in a field remotely similar to what I did in the Navy. They did not seem overly impressed with anything I had done, and I was not able to get many interviews. Those jobs seemed to be reserved for people with degrees rather than experience. I had no degree, so I had to take the first job I could get.

I went to work at a place making capacitors. I was operating an injection molding machine. I kept forgetting a step critical to the process, so they fired me after three weeks. This was the first time I had ever been fired. I felt very bad and rejected. I shrugged it off and had to look for another job.

I found my next job within a week, I hated this job more than any other job I ever had. I knew the minute I started there, I would not be there long. We received empty plastic barrels that had contained textile dyes. We cleaned and sterilized them, and then we would ship them back to the dye companies.

I worked third shift from 11 p.m. to 7 a.m. in the receiving department. This was the least preferred place in the whole plant. Our department began the process. When the barrels came in, they were covered, inside and out with whatever dye was originally put into them. My job was to pick up these big, heavy barrels, spray them out and put them on a conveyor. Once the conveyor was loaded, they would go through the rest of the sterilization process. Every night, I would be soaking wet and a different color. The job did not pay well either, but I needed a job. This job felt as if I were being punished. No one ever smiled, laughed or joked while at work. Turnover was also extremely high.

One afternoon the phone woke me up. It was my brother, Donald. He told me that my father had a heart attack and was at the hospital in Atlanta, Georgia. I left immediately to go see him. When I got there my dad was just sitting up in his bed and very happy to see me. He asked me how things were going. I lied and told him they were great. I did not want to give him anything to worry about.

I stayed in Atlanta for several days, and my father had angioplasty. The doctor said he was fine, and my dad told me he felt better than ever. I spoke to the doctor privately later and asked him what to expect for the future. He assured me if my father kept his stress down and ate right, with proper medication, he would live for many years. I decided I could do no more, and I went back home to South Carolina.

I did not even think to call my job before I left, and of course, they fired me. I didn't care. I was glad to never go back to that terrible place. I knew it wouldn't be long before I quit anyway. I didn't go back to work immediately. I had some money I had saved while I was in the Navy. I lived off it as I sat around for two weeks or so crying and worrying about my father. I called every day and would ask Dad how he felt. He assured me he felt fine, and it would not be necessary for me to worry about him.

During the next two years, I would have over forty different jobs. It was not hard to find a job in the southeastern United States at this time. Getting the job was never the problem. I spoke very well, and the people who I interviewed with would perceive me as highly intelligent. I would get hired on the spot most of the time. If I did not get hired right away, I would race home after the interview, so I would be there when the phone rang when they called to check references.

I had two phone numbers at home, and I would always make up a fake reference. If the reference phone rang, I would answer as whatever name I gave my interviewer, and I would always give myself a raving review. I would sometimes act excited that Tom Nardone was looking for work and ask them how to get in touch with him. I was hired often.

Shortly after getting a job I would find myself looking for a new one. Many times I was unable or unwilling to perform at the level I was expected to, and eventually I would be fired. Sometimes the job was just so boring I would just decide to quit. Depending on the place, my quitting would range from me giving a two week notice to just being annoyed and walking off the job quietly without saying anything to anyone.

I would then go to one of the five or six temporary agencies with which I had an account. They would usually have me in a new job within a day or two; sometimes the same day. So then, I started the process all over again. I remember there was one week I was fired twice. I had three different jobs within the same week.

At the end of one year, I went to have my taxes done, and I handed the lady 21 W-2 statements. She asked me, "What is this?"

I explained to her, "Ma'am I have had many jobs this past year." She was not happy about having to add twenty-one numbers up for every box on the tax form. It took some time, and she had no interest in small talk and exhibited no sense of humor while she was doing this. She asked me to go wait in the lobby because I think she didn't want to look at me.

I was fired for destroying furniture and other equipment with a fork lift. I was fired for coming in late. I was fired for low production level. I got fired for not staying late when they desperately needed me to. I was fired for the way I dressed. I was fired for things I said to my bosses. I lost count of all the places I worked.

One place I got fired because I did something just to see if I would get fired. On the way to work I got an idea, and I was simply curious. The building where I worked was very hot, as it had no air conditioning. The supervisor had an office in the middle of the plant. He sat on his fat ass all day in there with a window unit air conditioner. I resented the fact he was comfortable, and his window unit blew additional hot air into the plant, as if it wasn't already hot enough. I walked over and unplugged it while he was at lunch and opened his door. One of the people I worked with ratted me out to him, and he told me to get out.

I quit jobs for silly reasons. I quit one job because my boss was rude to me one day. I quit a job because it was too far to walk from the parking lot to my workstation. I quit a job because I did not like the music they played over the PA. I quit a job at a hotel because this man accused me of not putting in a wakeup call for him and caused him to miss his tee-time with the mayor. He accused me in front of my boss, who believed him without even questioning me. I told them both golf was a game for assholes anyway and walked off the property without a look in their direction. I quit one job because I had to sit in traffic for fifteen minutes every afternoon when I left to go home. The most badass time I quit a job was at a place where I made deliveries, and it was time to leave. I was heading to the time clock, and my boss said, "Not so fast, Tom."

I replied, "Excuse me?"

He said, "Hey, I need you to make another delivery before you go home."

I told him, "Sorry, I can't help you with that today."

He shouted, "Tom! Our delivery driver needs to be somebody who is flexible and does everything they can to make this company successful!"

I never once broke a step. I just kept walking as I said, "Well, silly you, I guess you should have hired that guy."

He said, "You are terminated."

I commented, "No shit."

I think I just didn't want to do any the jobs I would find, so I looked for some way, legitimate or not, to justify it. I rarely gave a notice, and many times I just walked off the job in the middle of the day, drove home and went to sleep without saying a word to anyone.

During this time in my life, I was also a sucker for every get-rich-quick scheme or multilevel marketing opportunity I saw. I had a job where I would carry a backpack around and sell knock-offs of name brand cologne and/or perfume to people on the street. I was involved with vitamin companies and any organizations where you try to get your friends involved doing stupid things such as these in order to make money without having to have a job.

My savings from the Navy eventually ran out, and I was making only enough money to cover bills. This brings us back to the beginning of my story. When Chet Smith fired me, and told about ADHD. I had no money, no food at home and many bills to pay. One of the things Chet said to me when he fired me was, "Find out what you want to do, and go do it better than anyone else." I had no money, and no job after I left Chet's office for the last time.

My net worth consisted of a full tank of gas in my car, and a bottle of ketchup in my refrigerator. I had finally hit bottom. I went out the following day and bought a newspaper and saw the job I knew was either going to make or break me. I decided I would try to get a job selling satellite dishes door-to-door.

I had always wanted to be in sales. I got to their office early the next morning, and I spoke with Bob, the sales manager. Bob was a really crabby bastard. He wasn't very personable. Bob did not really want to talk to me. I told him I was a go-getter.

Bob said, "No."

I asked him, "If I am only going to be paid for what I sell, then what do you have to lose?"

He said "No!" but I kept on talking. Finally, Bob said, "If you are not willing to take no for an answer from me, then I don't imagine you take a customer saying no for an answer either. Maybe you can do this."

Bob took fifteen minutes to explain the program to me, and I went out with ten blank contracts. I stayed out until almost 9 p.m. I came back that night with nine sales. Bob was locking the door when I got to the office. He was going home for the night, and he was in a bad mood because the whole office only turned in three sales for the whole day. I showed him the nine sales contracts I had, and he stared at them in silence. He looked at me and said, "Is this for real?"

I said, "Yes, of course it is."

Bob explained that since he had been working there he had never seen anyone turn in more than three contracts in a single day. He unlocked the door and told me to come in the office. He did not believe me. He told me if any of these contracts were false, I would be fired.

Bob faxed all nine apps in and said, "I will know in thirty minutes what the answer is." We sat there in his office in silence for almost an hour. The fax machine rang, and then began to spit out pages. Bob took each one and quickly looked at them as they came off the machine. When he had them all, he went back over them, but this time he was putting numbers in his calculator.

He looked and me and said, "Tom! You did great! You got nine approvals! How much money do you think you made, son?" It occurred to me we never discussed the pay structure. Bob said, "You made twelve hundred dollars today!" I just did not believe him, but he showed me. I asked him when I would get paid, and he told me it would be a week from today. I explained to him I was out of gas and had no money or food, so I would have to wait until next Monday to go back out to sell anything else. Bob said, "Come on, Tom. Let's go for a ride." Bob took me to dinner and filled my car with gas. He handed me two one hundred dollar bills and said please come back tomorrow, so I did.

I made very good money doing this. I was good at it, and I loved it. I really enjoyed going out and making a sale. It never got old. I later became the trainer and then the sales manager. I thought finally this is what I was meant to do. I figured I would do this for the rest of my life, but about eight months into it, the satellite companies started giving the dish for free and charging only for the programming. I was out of a job, again.

During this brief time of success, I met a girl named Dianne. I had always been afraid of young women. I would have never had the courage to ask a girl out. I ran an ad through a dating service, and she responded. She thought my ad was funny. In the "looking for" spot, it read, "SWF who is willing to lie about how we met". She answered, and we talked and decided to meet. We dated for a short time and eventually got married, and things were good for a while.

I went back to going from job to job again, but she had a steady job. I went to a place to sell computers through distribution channels. I did well at first, and I liked it. After a year being there I was relatively certain I would not be successful, so I quit and went to work for a company called RTI. I learned quickly it was an incredibly bad place to work.

My job was to get up every morning and put on a suit. I would then go, door-to-door, business-to-business and speak with business owners about switching their long distance service over to RTI. It was brutal. The first six months, I was to be on salary, then I was to live off the residual income from the commissions of the long distance bills of my customers. I gave it my very best for the first three weeks, but one morning my sales manager really pissed me off.

I decided to work from the phone one morning to cover more ground, and I was blown away when I finally got an appointment. It was just some piss-ant travel agent, who would not be a very lucrative customer, but at the time I had to take what I could get. I was very excited, and I could not wait to get off the phone and log it in my empty appointment book. As I got off the phone, my bosses Heath and Larry came into the office from their lunch break.

I said proudly, "Hey, Heath, I got us an appointment!"

To this he replied, "Well, it's about time. That is what you are supposed to do!"

Upon hearing this, I had no more motivation to do anything. The next day, Heath and Larry decided all three of us would go on my first appointment. The three of us entered, and I watched them gang up on this little man and browbeat the crap out of him in his office. They were like two used car salesmen. During their presentation, I noticed this man was so uncomfortable he could not even sit still. We left without the order, and Larry blamed me because I did not say a word while this idiotic display was unfolding. It was at that moment my daily routine at RTI would change dramatically.

I was for all practical purposes finished with RTI. I decided I would not talk to another company about their long distance service ever again, but I had a problem. I could not let my new wife worry I was without a job. I could not quit until I found something else. I would simply have to continue to work there until I was able to replace this job with a slightly-less-shittier one.

Monday morning, I went in at 8:00 a.m. After the morning sales meeting, I left to go out prospecting along with the other salespeople.

As I was about to enter my car, I noticed someone changing his clothes in his car. I walked over to the car and knocked on the window. When he rolled his window down, I asked him what he was doing. He explained he was going to his real job. He was just riding RTI out until his salary ended. I laughed so hard at this guy. He also said that he got this idea from two of the other sales people who had left before I ever got there.

Later, I found out that none of the current salespeople had ever posted a single sale there, and so obviously none of them had been there longer than 6 months. I also found out, our RTI office had been running for three years and posted a total of five sales. Five sales represented the entire production of this office. I decided then, this was a nowhere job.

It was clear they had very low expectations for their sales force. This was a total game changer for me. I was still pissed about Heath's attitude, and it made it very easy to decide what the rest of my days at RTI would entail. I decided I could just change my day around in such a way as to make everyone either happy or oblivious. My daily schedule would now be as follows:

> 7:30 am Put on my suit and leave my house.
> 8:00 am Attend morning sales meeting.
> 8:30 am Find some office park close by and write down the names of 30 to 35 businesses. Make up 30 to 35 first and last names of people I presumably spoke with. 9:30 am Go home and sleep for 6 or 7 hours 4:30 pm Wake up and put on my suit.
> 5:00 pm Go back to the office to attend the afternoon meeting.
> 6:00 pm End of a grueling workday.

Then, it was time to go home, see the wife and maybe watch some TV.

Sometimes, if I felt I didn't get enough sleep in the afternoon, I would call the office and say I was in a hot area, and I wanted to get some extra calls in for the day. I would avoid the afternoon meeting all together.

I would generally stay up all night playing games on my computer or cruising the internet until around 7:30 am when I would begin my fake workday and dress up for a meeting.

At the afternoon meetings, I would pull out my list of contacts for Heath or Larry to take and glance at so they could see how hard I had worked all day. The important thing here was to appear very enthusiastic about at least one of the people on my list. I kept a very positive attitude through all of this. I always appeared to be extra hopeful of one person on my list and would assure them this was a future client of RTI.

I did this for about four and a half months. At some point, I decided I should use my time to find a real job and prepare for my certain departure from RTI. Living this lie was without a doubt more exhausting then any job I had ever had before. It was so mentally exhausting I wondered if it was easier just going out and talking to people for real. I also did not like the way it made me feel. I know this was wrong, but I justified it by telling myself RTI should not have hired an asshole to run their sales office.

My last day with RTI, I went back to my old job where I sold computers for a visit. I hoped they would ask me if I wanted my old job back. They did ask me, and I agreed. I never even called or went back to RTI. I just stopped showing up for work and began my new job. They called the house looking for me, and Dianne told them that I started my new job. They were nice enough to mail me my final paycheck.

I was at my old job for one month. I gave it more of an effort than the first time I was there, but in spite of my efforts, they fired me for lack of performance. I decided I did not want to be in sales anymore. I was burnt out and tired of failing. I took a third shift job bending sheet metal and since they had no real expectations of any first year operator, I managed to get through it for a whole year.

I became good at it, but I hated it. I was too depressed about life in general to even look for another job, but I did want out of it. One day I got a call from The Home Depot. They offered me a job. I took it immediately. I liked these people, and they treated me well. I left notice, and two weeks later I started the last job I would ever have.

My life at home was worse than my professional life. I was learning Dianne was actually not the woman I thought I married. She was never satisfied with anything I did. She claimed to understand, but we fought constantly. I hated my life, and she was the main reason for it, but I was too afraid to be alone again. I made a commitment to her, and I would not leave her just so I could be happy. Being married to her was definitely a job, but not one I felt right about quitting.

Our fighting was the most ridiculous thing I had ever been involved with. She and I fought every single day. My father told me the day I got married, "Tommy, you are married now, and you have to make a choice. You can either be right or you can be happy. Choose the latter." I apparently heard him but did not listen. Our fighting had reached a particularly high pitch, and I reached out to my dad. I asked him was it normal for a husband and a wife to fight all the time about stupid stuff. I asked him, "Dad, when does the fighting end?"

My father replied, "Tommy, your mother and I have been married for twenty-seven years. I will let you know."

Over the years, Dianne and I had discussed the fact I was ADHD, and she had been pestering me to see a doctor and get on medication for it. I was always quitting or losing my jobs, and our bedroom was under renovations for the last three years. We lived in the guest room during this time. Dianne eventually won the doctor/medication battle, but not before a very dramatic event.

One Christmas Eve, we went to my parents' house, as we did every year. As soon as we got there, my mom started up about the clothes I was wearing. I don't know why this was a problem; I suppose she just wanted me to look nice for Christmas at her sister's house. As soon as my mom mentioned this, Dianne jumped on board and was seemingly enjoying giving me a hard time about this. This went on for twenty minutes or more. My mom asked me if she went out to the mall and bought me some clothes, would I wear them? I told her I would, and she went out on Christmas Eve to buy me clothes for dinner at her sister's house.

When Mom got back, I went to try them on, but they didn't fit. Mom finally just said. "Tommy, I am sorry. I am just glad you are here. You look fine." Dianne was not so apologetic. We went to dinner, and I managed to have a good time. In spite of the focus on my failure to please the women in my life with my fashion sense, or lack thereof, it went well, and I thought it was over.

As Dianne drove us home that night, she started in on the clothes again. She was driving, and she complained all the way from Atlanta to the South Carolina state line, without even taking a breath or pausing for me to say anything. I had my head leaned against the glass of the passenger's door, the whole time hoping a tractor-trailer would run us off the road and bring me sweet relief. I was not suicidal, but I was of the mind if there were a car destined to be run off the road, I was okay if our car was chosen.

As I sat there, I can remember being jealous of every person on earth that was dead. I thought, When I am dead I will have no responsibility and no one to disappoint. I thought it would be nice to be finished with my life. I thought it would be nice to join all the others who were experiencing the eternal sleep of the dead. I would not have to listen to this anymore, and I might not be so miserable.

We were on the road for an hour when she finally said, "Tom! Don't you even have one word to say to me?"

I just slowly turned my head toward her and said with no expression, "I'm sorry, were you talking?"

This was just what the doctor ordered. She finally shut her mouth, and we rode the rest of the way home in silence. It was a huge victory for me. It was no small thing to cause Dianne's mouth to close.

When we pulled into our driveway, she got out of the car and went into the house. She was absolutely furious. I didn't budge from where I was. I stayed in my seat, and continued to sit there with my head against the glass on Christmas Eve. I sat in the car by myself for two more hours, and then went inside and went to bed. The next morning we did not speak. My mom called and asked if everything was okay. I lied to her and told her it was. The silence went on until Dianne broke it later that afternoon when she informed me it was time to go.

We were going to her sister's house for Christmas dinner. I got ready and made a point to ask her to pick out my clothes, so as to avoid a repeat performance of the day before. She refused and told me a grown man should be able to dress himself. I got dressed and went into the den and sat down. I waited for her to finish so we could leave.

I was shocked when she came in and let out one of her dissatisfied sighs. My clothes, once again, just weren't good enough. She started up with me about what I was wearing to her sister's house. She was more hyped up then the night before with my parents. She asked, "What is wrong with you?"

I had always liked the term "bat-shit" when explaining someone has lost their mind or their composure. I always understood what was meant by it, but never so vividly as I did on this day when I went bat-shit.

At that moment, I hated everything and everyone in my life. I just wanted to disappear, so no one would ever see me again. I began screaming at the top of my lungs. I was not screaming words, it was just loud incoherent screaming. I chose the word screaming because yelling is not the correct word. It does not accurately describe my actions on this night. I was screaming. For about thirty seconds, I could not stop. I ran down the hall, and in mid-scream I kicked the door open to the guest room and jumped onto the bed and started having what I suppose was a nervous breakdown. The closest thing to describe my actions on the bed is to say it must have appeared as though I was having a seizure. I finally stopped and lay there, breathing heavy and fast. I was finally calming down.

Dianne got the message. She tried to forbid me going with her. Even though I did not want to go, I insisted on going for fear she would use this against me later in a future fight. We went to her sister's house late and had a quiet Christmas with them. We didn't speak a word the whole way there or the whole way home. She mentioned the idea of me seeing a doctor the next day, and I told her I would, even though I knew I wasn't going to do it.

At work the next day, I spoke to my friend and boss, Yvonne, about what happened. She said I should see about medication. She told me to go see a doctor because sometimes they prescribe medication and it helps. I was surprised to hear someone I respected agree with Dianne, but Yvonne just made sense when she explained it to me. I suppose it was because I knew Yvonne loved me and wanted only to help me, unlike Dianne. I finally agreed to stop fighting it.

I tried many things before I went on medication. I tried lists and all of the things people who are opposed to medication try. In addition to lists, I tried to read books and memory courses. I tried changing my diet and a host of other things people told me could help, but nothing was working. I was very anti-medication.

I went to the doctor, and I did not want to be there. I decided even before I met him he was an asshole. I went into his office, and he said, "Well, Mr. Nardone, what can I do for you?"

I simply said to him, "Sir, I would like you to write me a prescription for a pill that causes me to only hear things I give a shit about."

He laughed very hard and said my answer is the best one he ever heard. He then said, "Son, if I knew of such a pill, I would buy them all retire and never share one with anybody."

I laughed and that made me a little more open to what he had to say. It was determined after eight hours of testing, over the course of three days, I was ADHD and Bipolar. I scored a ten out of ten for ADHD, and an eight out of ten for Bipolar disorder. He said let's start by just treating you for ADHD. He referred me to the doctor who I still see today. He prescribed Adderall.

I had never taken any drugs in my life. I was not excited or anxious to get this prescription filled. I stuck it in my wallet and never said a word about it to anyone. In high school when my friends were doing drugs, I never one time tried any of them. My mother told me something years before that always stuck with me. She said, "Tommy, if you ever take drugs, it will break my heart." Anytime my saying no to my friends was not a sufficient, I would simply tell them, "It would break my mother's heart." It rarely went any further.

Dianne was pressuring me, so I got the prescription filled about four or five days later. I brought it home and sat in the den of my empty house, on the sofa, in total silence. I sat there staring at the container as it sat in front of me on the glass coffee table next to my water, and I began to think. I did not want to take this pill. I thought about how senseless it was that one of these tiny little pills could solve all my problems. A lifetime of pain, frustration and disappointment, and the answer is supposed to be in this little amber-colored bottle. It seemed silly to me.

As I sat in my den, that afternoon I thought about all the things I had tried in my life only to fall short of the mark. I thought about all the people that I had let down, while trying to make them proud and/or happy. I thought of all the jobs that fired me, when I believed in my heart I was doing well. I thought about my marriage that was destined to end. I thought about these and many other terrible things to which ADHD was linked or was the cause. All these things were true, but in spite of how awful my life had become or how many problems I had, one thing has always been true. I loved Tom Nardone.

As I sat on the sofa, I thought; I liked myself just fine, and I did not like the idea of taking a pill so that others would find me acceptable. I felt if this was the price of acceptance by the world, than the cost was more than I was willing to bear. I did not want to deal with the side effects of any of these medications. I did not want belong to a doctor's office for the rest of my life. I did not want to depend on this pill to fix me. I did not want to set up appointments or go to them. I did not want to talk to a doctor once a month. My so-called "ADHD" is a problem for them, not me.

My thoughts then halted, and I realized I was trying to talk myself out of this. I asked, *Why did Chet Smith, who would perhaps never see me again, take time to recommend this?* I asked myself, *Why did Yvonne tell me I should do this?* It occurred to me that they both cared about me enough to make an uncomfortable choice.

I suddenly began to see this in a different light. I realized I was not the only person this affected. It was everybody I loved and who loved me. I realized, I cared more about those people than I cared about myself. I am ADHD, not them. All of my failures and shortcomings made me feel bad over the years. I was tired of my family and the people I loved having to watch me fail over and over. My shortcomings were also a source of pain for the people I cared about; I did not want to disappoint them anymore.

While I did not believe the answer was in that little amber bottle, I decided that if I did nothing, then nothing would happen. If I tried something different, maybe things would change. I thought if it didn't work, I could always stop. What is the harm in trying it?

I picked up the bottle and took out a single pill. I put it on my tongue and drank it down with a glass of water. This moment marked the beginning of my treatment.

Chapter 11

A few seconds after taking my pill, I rolled my eyes, and thought about how silly the whole thing was, but fifteen minutes later, while there was no physical feeling, I did notice two changes. I noticed the absence of a fog in my head. I was not even aware of it ever being in my life until it was gone. It just seemed to vanish. I had a very strange and unfamiliar sense of alertness. I had an immediate feeling I was now able to do things. I just felt right and in control.

The other change, which was far more noticeable, was the absence of my irritability. I remember feeling happy, and I was not worried about anything. I started cleaning the kitchen. This was something I would have never taken the initiative to do. I never cleaned the kitchen unless Dianne said to do so, but I cleaned it to perfection. I went on to do other things around the house and completed them all.

While I was cleaning the house, I could not get past how my irritability was not present. I was trying to think of a way to put this to the test when it occurred to me the most irritating part of my life would be home from work soon, and for the first time in years, I could not wait until my wife came home. I was not afraid. I just wanted to see if her nagging would be a match for my new medication. I was so excited when I heard her car pull into the driveway. She got home, but she did not nag me as I had hoped she would. I think I got so much work around the house done she was just in too good of a mood.

I was stuck on this being irritated test, and then it occurred to me. The thing I hated the most was when she would start talking about her day. This was always a gut-wrenching endurance test that would have an atheist praying to God for its end. The thing I feared the most was for her to come home and begin a conversation by saying, "You won't believe what happened at work today."

After the shock of my cleaning the house wore off, I asked her to please tell me about her day. She went on and on and on, and I found myself listening to her. I was no more interested in what she said than I ever was, but I had a new-found ability to stomach every bit of her nonsense. I tried to keep it going as long as I could just to see if I had a limit to the amount of bullshit I could listen to. As it turned out, my ability to listen exceeded her ability to give it. There was no fighting, and there was no drama. I kissed her later that evening and left to go to work.

I got to work, and things were different there, too. I started working right away. Normally, I would just stand around with everybody else and do nothing until Yvonne would tell us where to go work. I did not wait for instructions. I knew what needed to happen, and I got busy working on it. Yvonne and my coworkers wondered what happened to me, and I told them about my medication. I was not ashamed; I was proud. None of them could keep up with me that night. I was like a brand new employee who works hard all night because they don't know any better. Other things in my life changed as well.

While I was in the Navy, I bought a guitar and thought I would learn to play. I played the classical/Spanish guitar. I learned four songs I could play well during the time I was in the Navy, but I could not seem to learn any new songs. As I would try to learn a new song, I would determine it was just too difficult. This went on for ten years. I would try to learn a new one, but after five or ten minutes, I would think it was just too hard and go back to the same four songs I knew I could play. After my ADHD was treated, within six months, I added sixteen songs in my repertoire. I played two weddings and a coffee bar to the applause of hundreds.

Many things improved in my life. Many things changed. The best way to explain it is to say this: Oil will not prevent engine parts from rubbing together, but it will make it easier. The engine will do more work, and it will be far more dependable. That is a fair assessment of what my medication did for me. The day I ingested that little orange pill was the day that I figuratively emerged from my past failures. I was excited about my new life. I was curious everyday how I would do it better.

After a while, the excitement did wear off, but I was still light years ahead of where I was before taking medication. Dianne's excitement wore off as well, and she manifested this through complaining. Once I began being more productive, she decided to raise the bar. She would mock and ridicule me for not doing enough. This was still very hard to hear, and prior to being treated for my ADHD, I would grovel on the ground at her every disappointment while crying. I became as humble as a whipped puppy, and I considered myself just a shell of a man. Now, things were different.

Dianne continued giving me problems, but my medication helped me use my brain to come up with more creative forms of problem-solving. Where I was once only reactive, I could now be proactive. What I once considered an imminent and unavoidable defeat, I now sought after victory.

I considered my wife a bully, and I decided I wasn't going to take it anymore. For me our marriage had become a game of winning and losing, and I wanted to win. I always heard people say winning isn't everything, but I never heard the winners saying this. This was one of my first marital victories.

We had had a 600-square foot addition added to the back of our house that would later become our master bedroom. What I had planned to finish in just three to four months, ended up taking about four and a half years. I'm ADHD, and my favorite days of the week were tomorrow and that day I set aside to do important things in my life. I was about three years into the project, and of course, I was not finished. With the help of my medication, I was making considerable progress.

The problem came one spring. Dianne had been raising hell for so long about the addition being finished, but I was finally working on it. So, she decided she wanted the yard to be nice this year as well. One thing you need to know about Dianne and yard work is Dianne did not do yard work. Aside from planting a few flowers now and then, she did nothing. She wanted our yard to look nice, but not at the inconvenience of depriving our sofa the joy of having her ass spread out on it while she watched reruns of her favorite TV shows all day long.

Her plan was for me to be outside working in the yard all day, and working on the addition all night. I knew my wife, and I knew, just like a day-killing freight train, she would never stop. I was not flexible on this. I knew the yard was off the table, and it was not going to happen.

I hit "The Misery Trifecta": a nagging wife, an incomplete house addition and now a yard to give a shit about after years of blissful neglect by the both of us. All of my free time was in jeopardy, and now, I would not even be able to look forward to the weekends. The only thing I knew was that there was no way I was going to do all of this. There was one thing different. I was on my medication. The old Tom Nardone would have reasoned, talked, pleaded and then lost this discussion. I would have submitted to her whims and ultimately disappointed her with a failing attempt.

Things were now different. The fog in my mind had lifted. They say clearer heads prevail. My head was clear, and it was time for me to prevail. She wanted something done; believe me, something was going to be done.

Two whole days passed, without a word of this coming up again. Sunday night, just before she went to bed, I said, "Hey, honey, I thought a great deal about what you said about the yard, and you know, you're right. I am going up to Home Depot and figure out what we need to do to fix our yard."

She was so happy. I actually even went outside, and (just for show) I dug up a sample of our yard to show the people at Home Depot, so they could "help" me. She thought it was great. I got in my car and left. As soon as I cleared our street, I tossed the dirt sample out of my window.

When I got to Home Depot, I asked my friend, Mike in the garden department, if he wouldn't mind helping me:

> Mike: What can I do for you, Tom?
> Me: I need to buy something to spray on my lawn that will kill every weed, every blade of grass and every living thing in it.
> Mike: Excuse me?
> Me: Shall I repeat what I said?
> Mike: You want to kill... the lawn?
> Me: Winner!!!
> Mike: Okay, uh, how big is your yard?
> Me: Half an acre.
> Mike: One of these bottles should do one acre. Me:
> Great, I'll take two.

When I got home my wife was in bed, but I was so excited that I couldn't even wait until morning. I got my sprayer and my death concoction, mixed at double strength, and sprayed the entire backyard twice. It felt great.

I was walking up and down our yard with my pump sprayer, showering the lawn I hated with liquid death. I was coughing and trying to stay upwind. The hardest part was trying not to laugh while I was doing it. My wife worked Monday through Friday. She left the house at 6:00 a.m., and she got home at 5:30 p.m. She would not be home during the daylight hours until Saturday morning.

I couldn't believe how fast it worked. Each day our yard looked deader than the day before. By Friday afternoon, it was dead. I mean like post-apocalypse, tombstone, tumbleweeds and old western TV show dead. For five days, I watched my lawn die a slow death, and I could not have been more pleased with myself.

Friday night I went to work. It was just a few short hours until the big reveal with Dianne. I worked third shift, and that night it occurred to me half way into my shift, in all the excitement, I had not thought about what I would tell my wife. I began to think and think some more. I thought about it all night. I got my friends involved, but all they could do was laugh. They tried to convince me there was no way out.

After my shift, I drove home and quietly walked around the side of my house into the backyard. I actually hoped it would be alright, but no, the grass was still dead. I thought some more about it, but I decided it would just be best to come clean. I tried, I failed and now I must face the music. There was a door into the bedroom off the back deck, so I walked up to the door ready to admit my wrongdoing and my underhandedness. When my fingers touched the door, I had what alcoholics refer to as a moment of clarity. This moment of clarity was something like this.

I thought, *What am I doing? Am I about to surrender and admit defeat to a dead lawn? Of course, my friends told me I was going to be in the doghouse. That is how their minds work. Most people would see this situation as a death sentence; whereas, I, on the other hand, will transform this would-be disaster into the stage on which I shall steal the hearts and minds of my audience. Let the show begin.*

Lights, Camera, Action!

(An angry Tom Nardone walks onto the scene)

"Dammit Dammit Dammit! What the hell? Son of a bitch!" I shouted at the top of my lungs.

My wife, hearing my rage, came outside and asked, "What's the matter, Tom?"

I said, "What's the matter? Look at my yard, just look at it. I killed the whole thing. It's all dead! I sprayed it with weed and grass killer. This is what the guy at Home Depot recommended. All that work, and now look at it."

I then kicked something off the porch and knocked over a broom.

She said, "Hey, sweetie, calm down, calm down. You tried. This is not your fault. It will grow back, and look, you will be able to focus on the addition this summer."

I said, "Are you sure you're not mad?"

She said, "No. I'm not mad."

I said, "Okay, just give me a minute out here, and let me calm down."

She said, "Okay, I will go make some coffee."

I said, "Thanks for not being mad, babe."
She said, "Don't worry about it, sweetie," and she went inside.

With no rehearsal, no second takes and no script, I was the writer, producer and director of a larger-than-life production. I did what would have undeniably brought Broadway to its knees, and I did it on the fly.

This scheme had a two-pronged effect. First, I got out of doing any yard work for the entire spring and summer. Second, every time my wife saw the yard, she was reminded that I cared enough to try to make a difference. As it turned out, she was right. I made a tremendous difference, especially when the wind blew, and you could not see across the backyard through the clouds of dust.

I do not dispute what I did was deceptive; however, if you will review the text, at no time did I ever lie to her. I was clear as to what I sprayed on the lawn. I said to her I would "fix" our yard. We certainly had different ideas about what that meant. The only other things I said to her about it was "look at the yard, I killed it. The whole thing is dead", and "this is what the guy recommended" all of which was true.

I did not review my actions and figure out what we talked about and come up with some lie. I did not put these things in reverse and try to work backwards. I just used the momentum I already established to gracefully cruise across the finish line. I shifted it into overdrive, put the pedal to the floor and gave the performance of a lifetime. If I had come clean with my wife, she would have been mad, I would have worked all summer.

I do consider this a victory, but I don't mean to say my medication fixed this or any of my problems. Let me be clear about one thing. Medication has not fixed a single one of them. I am an adult with ADHD. The medication just makes the symptoms manageable and helps me. There are certain things I am able to do I could not do before. The things I could do before, I do much better, while I am on my medication.

A successful marriage with Dianne was never going to happen. The amount of medication it would have taken to allow me to enjoy being around her would have literally killed me. I would need some kind of drug in a liquid form, administered through an I.V. and a backpack to carry it.

Even though I had decided not to be her lapdog any longer, I did want to do what I could to keep the peace. I wanted our marriage to work even though I didn't believe it would. While I was no angel and I brought plenty of problems to our marriage, she had quite an arsenal of her own.

Dianne worked at a group home for sexually-abused, teenage girls. She worked with a staff, composed entirely of women. One day while they were all at work, they decided it would fun for all of them to go out and have dinner. I would have been elated to hear of her spending all night away from our house, but they also decided it would be fun to bring their husbands.

Now things took a turn for the worst, as I now had to leave the comfort of my home. I had to support this ridiculous endeavor. She called me at home and told me to start getting ready. I tried to get out of it, but she assured me all of the women were bringing their husbands. When she told me this, I really did not want to go.

We went to a place I had been to before. I did like the place, but I could not stand Dianne's coworkers. My presence was mandatory. Two things I could not stand were to have a place I had to go and a time I had to be there. I just figured I would have to write off at least five hours off my life, as I would never get them back. It was not just dinner, and this particular place did a show after dinner was served.

I did not believe I was going to have a good time, decided I would try my best to keep the peace and not embarrass Dianne. I just accepted there was no way out of this trip to "Hell's Museum of Disappointments". It was unavoidable.

Of course, we were the first to arrive. We sat down, and, one by one, these women showed up and did so without their husbands. Only one other woman was able to con her husband into this evening's delights. The women were loud and completely unaware of themselves. I was actually embarrassed, and it took a hell of a lot to embarrass me.

All seven of us were there, and during a brief pause in the ladies' cackling laughter, I leaned over to the other moron who could not stand up to his wife and told him I was going to the bar to get a beer and asked if he would like me to get one for him. He said, "No, my wife doesn't let me drink." So now, it was official. I hated every person at the table.

The worst thing about the whole evening was listening to the conversation at our table. They talked shop, and their conversation went to every place it should not have. They spoke of the abuse experienced by the girls in their care. They spoke of all kinds of feminine issues. The conversation even covered penis sizes; length and girth.

I sat the whole time wondering why I was there. I did not speak all night long. Nobody asked me a thing, and I could not have been happier about it. I went back to get another beer for myself. When I returned the show had begun. I did not enjoy the show because when I came back to sit down at the table, Dianne gave me the cold stare. This meant we were going to have a bad car ride back to the house.

As prophesied, we had a bad car ride back to the house. I remember her main complaint was I did not speak to any of her friends. I knew this was an argument I was not going to win. The only way to win was to make her so mad, she couldn't talk. It is this tactic, which I used to end this insanity. I was tired of these bad car rides, and I had had my fill. It seemed as though everywhere we ever went we always took "Hell's Locomotive" to get there. I was not about to let the conductor punch my ticket. Instead, I would lay my own tracks and illustrate the absurdity, with absurdity.

I said, "Darling, you are right, and I am sorry. When you gals started discussing penis sizes, I just really should have spoken up. I mean, I have a penis, and the other husband at our table clearly did not. I really think that I should have contributed more to the conversation. Even if I did not have anything to say I could have at least cared enough about you and your friends to give you all a visual aid for the purpose of your discussion. Listen babe, next time we are out with your friends at dinner, I will begin the conversation by standing up and whipping it out for everyone's close and thorough inspection." Problem solved; Dianne had nothing more to say.

We rode home in a blissful silence. Tom Nardone wins again.

Not all of Dianne's complaints were unwarranted. There are things that a woman expects from a marriage. I get this. I was not the ideal husband. My intentions were good most of the time, but sometimes the results of my excitement cast a shadow and concealed my intentions. My excitement often prevented me from seeing the big picture.

While I gave up on the idea of us ever being happy, I never gave up on the whole marriage. Dianne and I had an anniversary coming up. This was our fifth anniversary, and I had forgotten a couple of them in the past. I wanted to do everything I could to make this a special day, and a day she would not forget.

The night before our anniversary my boss, Yvonne, and I ran to Wal-Mart during our lunch break at 1:00 a.m. I bought gifts and decorations. This was going to make up for all the anniversaries that I had forgotten in the past. When I got home that morning, she had already left for work. I began hanging streamers. I made a sign. I wrapped the gifts in a beautiful paper I chose, and I did it ever so carefully. I finished very quickly and decided I would make a nice dinner. I ran to the store and bought everything I needed to make her favorite spaghetti my father had taught me to make.

I had finished ahead of schedule, so I thought I would take a nap. I got a few hours of sleep, and my alarm went off. I jumped up, made the bed and checked on the dinner, which was perfect. Dianne called and said she would be running about thirty minutes late. I said fine and told her I would see her when she got home. I would have to wait an additional thirty minutes. Finally, I saw her headlights shine through the dark den, and her motor shut off. She came to the door and opened it.

She was so surprised. She walked in, and I could see that she was more than surprised. She walked through the gauntlet of anniversary decorations I had worked so hard to prepare. She got to the kitchen where her gifts were, and she carefully looked at all I had prepared for her. She went back into the den from the kitchen to look at the sign I made that read, "Happy Anniversary". She was not smiling, but I thought she was just overwhelmed. I realized she was not overwhelmed as her expression quickly turned to anger. I looked at her and asked, "Is something wrong, dear?"

Her response was, "No, there is nothing wrong, I guess, except my dumb ass of a husband doesn't seem to know or care what day we got married."

I said, "It is the fifth, and today is the fifth."

Apparently, we were married on the fifteenth. She was furious. She then began to shout at me, "You can take all of this shit back where you got it! I don't want it!" She went to the bedroom, and I did not see her for the rest of the evening except when she came out to make herself a sandwich. She made a peanut butter and jelly sandwich right by the spaghetti she could clearly see I had made for us. She did this just to further illustrate her disappointment in me.

I felt bad at first and tried to apologize and told her it was just a simple mistake, but my words had no value to her. My regret just turned to anger, and I just said to hell with it. I calmed down and sat down and enjoyed my spaghetti while I sat in the den and enjoyed both of the movies I rented for us to watch.
I know I really screwed up, but she acted as if I forgot it. What made me so mad was my intentions were noble, and I felt that Dianne could have chalked this up to my ADHD, and just said, "Oh, Tom."

This incident did not have to be a dramatic one. She did not appear at any time to be hurt. I think the irony of this evening is Dianne received from me the greatest gift a person such as herself could ever receive. She was given something to bitch about.

This disaster did not end there. Ten days later when our actual anniversary came up, I screwed that up, too. I remembered it, but I thought she was so mad about my previous debacle she did not want to hear another word about it. I was of course wrong about this, too. She got plenty of mileage out of this as well. She raised hell for an hour. So, Dianne, for a second time, received her favorite thing which she loved more than anything else in her life.

My marriage was all but finished, but I had become accustomed to this. Everything else in my life was going well. I was doing well at my job, I was getting things done on the addition to our home and the yard required absolutely no maintenance whatsoever. For the first time in my life, I was mostly happy. I felt like I could do anything. I believed there was nothing I could not handle. This new found life of mine would soon be put to the ultimate test.

Chapter 12

I decided to go back to school and see about getting some training to get a better job. I thought I wanted to be in the IT field. I signed up and was attending to get a certification in web design. It was a very small school. The people at the school and I became friends instantly. I excelled so much at web design they offered me an internship to be their web designer.

The school was moving and needed help renovating the new building. I had all the necessary skill sets for the tasks. They asked me for my help, and I was happy to oblige them. They were all good people, and we really became a sort of family. I spent a great deal of my time off helping get this place get ready.

I was working one Sunday morning, and I took a break and called my parents' house, as I often did. My dad answered the phone, and he was in a particularly good mood. He and I were laughing and joking as we always did when the two of us got to talking.

We talked for a while and my father asked me what I was planning on doing that day. I told him I was helping some people out who ran the school I was attending get some things done so they could open on time. My father was moved by my willingness to do this for them.

Dad started talking to me about my life, and he said. "Tommy, do you know how proud of you I am? You are out there, and you are just doing it. You never ask us for anything, and I am just so proud of you and the man you have become, but I am just proud of the way you live your life. You are a fine son, and I love you so much."

It seemed just a little out of context, but I was glad to hear this from my father. I said, "Dad, I am glad you are proud of me. I have always wanted your approval in everything that I did."

Dad said, "Okay, Tommy, I am taking the jet ski to the lake today. I will talk to you later, and I am sorry, son, but I just wanted you to know that I love you and that I'm proud of you."

I said, "It's no problem, Dad. I know you are, and I love you, too."

It was a Sunday night, Dianne and I had just finished dinner and were about to watch the only show we could watch together: Law and Order: Criminal Intent. It was just about to come on, and the phone rang. It was Donald. He was frantic, he said, "Tom, Dad is okay for now they are working on him. He was on his jet ski today, and they think he had a heart attack, but they are working on him. I am at the hospital with Mom and everybody."

I just said, "Okay, Donald." He hung up fast, and I sat on the floor where I was standing and stared at the phone, as I silently hoped for it not to ring.

Donald called me back ten minutes later and said, "Tommy, Dad's gone, brother. He's gone." In the background, I heard the worst sound I had ever heard in my entire life. It was the sound of my mother screaming out in pain. It seared into my memory. None of this seemed real.

I very calmly said, "Donald, I am on my way. Tell everyone, I am on my way."

I looked at Dianne, and said, "My father is gone." I almost lost it for a moment. I contained my rage, but my tears escaped. I did not accept it right away. I had spent the last nine years imagining this day ever since my father had his heart attack. It was strangely much as I imagined it would be. All I could think about was how something must not be right about all of this because I was not ready to lose my father that day.

The car ride to Atlanta that night was a blur. It was late when we got there, and there was no place to park at my parents' house. Every member of our family was there. I walked up the steep driveway and into to the saddest room I ever saw. At that moment, it all became real for me. At that moment, I accepted that my father was gone; the best friend I ever had was gone. My hero was gone.

The man that took me to T-ball practice and worked multiple jobs so I would be taken care of was gone. The man who took me to work with him so I could learn my multiplication tables was gone. The man who, even though he yelled at me, always came back afterwards and sat down beside me and put his loving arms around me to make sure I knew he still loved me was gone. I would never again hear his beautiful voice. My hero was dead.

The only thing that had sustained me through my years with Dianne was the fact I could call my father anytime and speak with him. He had an amazing insight, and he was always so calm and diplomatic about the way he dealt with anyone who asked him for help. This was gone too now. I would not have anyone to help me solve the problems in my life as only he could. I would not have anyone to ask to help me fix things when I could not figure them out. I did not know what I was going to do without him.

In spite of all the bad things I felt toward Dianne, she was a godsend to my family through all of this. She helped around the house with meals and with funeral arrangements. She was a strong person, and she really stepped up to help my family when we needed her. She also did love my father.

I was in Atlanta for a week. As traumatic as this was, I accepted the loss of my father, and I was doing pretty well under the circumstances. The hardest part for me was seeing the faces of my family. Seeing my mom and my brothers was the most difficult part. I am the oldest son, and I felt like I should have answers for them. They looked at me, and I had nothing for them.

My uncle, Steve was taking it bad also. I had never seen him sad before. Dad was his big brother, and they were very tight. Steve loved his big brother, and it was not easy to see him this way.

Nobody, and I mean nobody, took this as hard as my mother did. She needed me to be around her, and I was through the whole process. My family was emotionally crippled at the loss of my father. He was loved by us all.

I had never experienced a close family member passing. My father's wake was my first wake. The funny thing I learned about wakes is they are sad at first, as you might expect, but after a while you can hear people laugh. You know why you're there, but you forget until someone else shows up and then it gets sad again.

I dreaded going to the wake, but at times it was fantastic. I listened to stories about my dad, stories I had never heard before. I could not get enough of them. I was sorry when the wake ended. I wanted to stay but after four hours, the crowd began to thin out and we went back to the house.

At the funeral, three of us were to give a eulogy: Uncle Steve, Donald and me. Donald, bless his heart, could not bring himself to speak. He tried, and I believed my dad would have been proud. Donald, like me, looked up to my father and always wanted to be the person my dad was. He went to the podium and then stepped away quietly, and deferred to me.

I began by asking the entire room to raise their hands if they can recall my father ever showing up to their home with his tool belt to fix something that had broken. I believe there were probably over seventy-five hands up in the crowd. They began to laugh because few were aware of the number of lives he had touched. I told stories and quoted my father without shedding a tear. During my eulogy, people were laughing out loud, and it was the eulogy I believe my father would have wanted to hear from his son.

My mother very unexpectedly got up when we were finished and said she would like to speak on her husband's behalf as well. She spoke of doing it that morning, but I don't know if anyone believed she would be able to do it. My mother got up from her chair and walked up to the podium. I will never forget the courage of my mother. She got up there and spoke elegantly of the greatest man she had ever known.

She had much to say. She spoke of how they met and stories from their high school days. She did so with great strength and conviction, as she honored her late husband, and when she was finished, the only dry eyes were her own. I was never more proud of her than on that day. When I saw her up there, I was no longer scared of living without my hero, and I knew we were all going to be going to be okay.

We spoke of the man, the father, the brother, the husband, and of the hero, we lost.

I was out of work for two weeks. I came back home and spent a great deal of time at the school trying to stay busy. Working at my school and fixing things were actually a nice distraction. The best way I knew to handle these things was for me stay busy. I stayed busy constantly. I worked twelve-hour days at the school.

People say you never get over certain things, and I guess they are right. You do learn to move on though. Prior to the passing of my father, I would have told you on the day he died, my life would also end. It did not end, but in many ways, it had just begun.

Chapter 13

Things were difficult for a while after the passing of my father. I found myself at a place where I could not figure something out. I moved toward the phone, as I always did, to call and ask my father for his advice, but only then realized, this was no longer an option. I did the best I could, and I just wondered what my father's opinion of it would have been. I felt I could never ever again have his approval. I had to figure things out by myself for the rest of my life. My mother was there for me, and I loved her for it. I just wanted my dad back, too.

During the time shortly after my father passed, things between Dianne and me were civil. They slowly went back to what I knew as normal. Dianne and I had planned to go see my mother one weekend. Things were getting worse for my mom. She could not focus on anything except her husband was gone. At the last minute, Dianne backed out of the trip and said, "Tom, why don't you go see your mom without me and spend some time with her." She did not have to ask me twice. I could always use a break from Dianne.

Not wanting to leave Dianne stranded, I rented a car and left on a Friday afternoon and planned to stay until Sunday. I had a nice visit with my mom, and on Sunday night I was about to head home. Before I left Mom's house I wanted to let Dianne know I was on my way home, so she didn't freak out when she heard me come in late, but I got no answer. I had tried to get in touch with her several times during the day, but I just could not connect with her.

As I drove home, I pondered how strange it was for Dianne not to pick up the phone. She was always home, and I could not imagine where she could possibly be. This got me thinking, and I began to wonder about a lot of other things she had said and done over the past couple of months. I realized she had not called to check on me or to ask about my mom. She had opened a savings account, and I saw an apartment finder magazine in our home around this time. These thoughts began to race, and it occurred to me perhaps she left.

I thought about the possibility she may have left me. I started to believe she did, and I imagined this Dianne-free-fantasy to make the car ride more enjoyable. The idea of life without her intrigued me, and I could not get this out of my mind. I was no longer thinking about whether she left, but about what life without her would be like. I kept thinking about it and smiling, but I knew I would be stuck with her forever. I would not have ever left her. I did not stay with her because

145

I lacked the balls to leave, even though I did lack the balls. I did not stay with her because I didn't have the initiative to leave, even though I didn't have it. I stayed with her because I had made a commitment.

The closer I got to my house the more excited I became. I was driving faster than I normally would have. I was talking to myself in the car on the way home. I was saying aloud, "Come on, woman, do something good for me for once. Please, be gone when I get home!" As I crested the hill on our street, my mailbox came into view in the low lights of the street lamps. Something was askew, but I could not figure out what I was looking at until I got closer.

On February 29, 2004, as I pulled into my driveway, there were about fifteen bags of garbage in front of the house, and the driveway was empty. I frantically tried to open the front door, as I fumbled with my keys. I walked in the front door, and the house was clean and uncluttered. I remember I had not seen the house look so good in quite a while. I slowly walked through the house and looked around just to sort of take everything in. I also had to be certain she did not take any of my things.

When I entered the master bathroom I noticed some items neatly placed on the vanity. Among them was a brief note explaining everything. I read the note and began to smile, and then I began to laugh. This was followed by yelling. I was not yelling in a bad, oh-my-god way. I was yelling the same way I yell before an epic rock concert begins. I laughed, and I laughed. I was free. When I calmed down, I said out loud, "Ding Dong, the witch is dead."

I called my mother to tell her the good news. She was the only one who was upset about this. I found this a little strange. She hated Dianne. Mom hated the way she treated me. I told her I was thrilled about my life without Dianne.

I really was ecstatic. The shackles were gone. I would not have to answer any more questions such as, "Have you been smoking?" "Have you been drinking?" "How much longer are you going to be on that computer?" "When is this going to be done?" "Where you going with those people?" "When are you going to be home?" "Are you listening to what I am saying?"

I did not have to ever again answer to her for anything I ever did for the rest of my life, ever! I remember the first rule I broke that night. I went out and got a pack of cigarettes and smoked them in the house. I walked through every room with a cigarette, and I felt great about blowing smoke all over the house.

The only thing worried about was it was Sunday night, and *The Sopranos* were coming on soon. Less than an hour after I found out my wife had left me, the most important thing to me was not missing *The Sopranos*. That was a quick recovery. I could barely pay attention to my show. All I could think about was how free I was and how I now finally had a chance to be happy.

Life with Dianne was a tragic tale of misery. As long as I was down, she did not feel so small. She mocked me at everything I tried. She made no attempt to help me or be a part of anything I did for us. I was a husband, reduced to a shell of a man, while she spent the seven years of our marriage with her ass spread out on the sofa.

Every time I came home from anywhere, I was nervous. I wondered what she might have found or seen that would bring questions to her mind with which to interrogate me. It happened more times than not. Coming home to my house was always a scary thing for me.
Everything I did, and everything I didn't do, was fuel for her inferno of insults, ridicule and hate that burned within her heart. I could not believe I was free from her, and this consumed my thoughts.

I had no idea that night how I was going to pay bills, go to work or survive, and I did not care. None of the logistics of this change even occurred to me. I could only think about one thing. I was free. While she took almost all of the money and the only car we had, I bounced back quickly. I had a few side jobs I completed, and I got a car for myself within a week. As far as the rest of the money she stole from me, I managed to get the books balanced and then some.

Dianne had given her last instructions to me, and I decided nobody was ever going to lead me around by the nose again. I decided I was in charge of my life from now on. I was going to answer only to those I wanted or chose to answer to. I could do whatever I wanted to do for the first time in my life.

Even with medication, I just could not take the nagging every day and the whining and the complaining. It was too much. I had tried to live my life the way I thought would please others for almost all of my life, and I was ready to stop this. I wanted to do what I wanted to do, and I did not want to explain myself to anyone. I did not want to share the things I think or believe with someone who I had to worry was going to get mad about them.

147

I think the secret to any marriage whether ADHD is in it or not is to simply ask yourself can you accept this person the way they are today. If there is anything you are hoping will change in someone, you will most likely be disappointed.

ADHD did not kill my marriage. Marriage is a commitment between a man and a woman. Not a man, a woman and an acronym. I was very irritable all the time, and I had the wrong wife. I admit I played my part in what destroyed us, and I did nothing constructive to save it. I was just not interested in it anymore. For me, it became all about something else. It was not about love or the promise I made. It became about me not losing. I was tired of losing.

It took me over thirty years to make this decision, but I am done worrying about whether or not the way I live my life makes people feel. There is not a person on this earth I need that badly.

Chapter 14

The night following Dianne's departure, I called my best friend, Yvonne. I told her the news. I invited her over, and we talked for a while. I always loved Yvonne, and I really thought it was a shame I was married to Dianne. I often thought, if Yvonne and I were together, my life would be so much better. I knew I would never leave my wife, and I knew that Yvonne would never want to be with me, so I just wrote it off in my head as a silly pipe dream or a fantasy.

Yvonne and I talked for a while, and she indicated to me she was not happy with where her life was. Admittedly, I was encouraged by this. She left that night, and I went to bed. The next morning I woke up and could not stop thinking about her. I thought maybe Yvonne and I needed the same thing. Maybe what both of us needed was each other.

When we worked together on the night shift, we would sit in our cars and talk for an hour or more. I would call Yvonne on the weekends to see how things were going for her as she was in a similar unhappy place as I was. She was the reason I stayed at the job. I loved having her as a boss. Seeing her attitude at work taught me so much about a work ethic and about integrity. The only person I ever knew who had a more profound effect on my life was my father. I always loved Yvonne.

For days, I wrestled with if I should tell her how I felt. I went back and forth and could not decide if I should risk our friendship by saying something to her. I confided in a friend of mine at work. After talking with him all night, I decided not knowing if she would care how I felt was going to be much harder to live with than the possibility of losing her as a friend.

I invited her over a couple of nights later to watch a TV show. After the show, she was getting up to leave, and I asked her to wait. She sat back down. I explained to her how I felt and I told her I loved her and that I always have loved her. She could not believe it. She was speechless, and I knew I had gone too far. I told her I was sorry and to please just forget it. She remained speechless for a moment, but then confessed to me that she had always felt this way about me. I asked her if I could kiss her, and she asked me, "Well, what if it is weird?"

I said, "Then, I will put a funny movie on, and we will watch it and forget it ever happened."

She said, "Okay."

It was not weird at all. It was awesome. We did not watch a movie, rather talked about the future as we were both so happy because we knew then we were going to be in each other's lives forever. When Yvonne left, I could not believe it. I did not sleep at all. All I thought about was how Yvonne and I would be together. I had no doubt I would someday marry her.

Being with Yvonne also meant being with a nine-year-old kid named Brett. Brett was her son and a unique child. I never had kids, and I always thought I would never marry a woman who did. I knew I wanted to spend the rest of my life with Yvonne, and her having a child would not discourage me.

I had met Brett a few times while we were dating. We knew each other's names, and we had small talk here and there, but neither of us knew the other one very well. We had not yet bonded.

Yvonne was working, and she had a crazy schedule. She could not be home every day when Brett got home from school. It became routine for me to go to her house when I got off of work. Each day when Brett came home, he came charging into the house, slamming the front door behind him. He ran across the den and put his book bag on the kitchen table. As he ran back to the steps to go to his room, the only thing on his mind was playing his video games.

Every day as Brett ran up the steps, he would stop and ask if I wanted to watch him play his video game. Every day, I told him I was not really into video games, and he said, "Okay," and went about his business. This happened for a while until one day Brett said, "Tom, don't you even want to watch me play? You can just watch me you don't have to play." It occurred to me Brett was reaching out to me, and I was rejecting him. I wanted to get to know him better, and I felt I should try to take an interest in what was important to him.

I told him, "Eh, why not?" and I went up the stairs with him. The last time I played a video game was many years before. After watching for only a moment, I could not believe how far video games had advanced. I was watching him play this game, and I was blown away by the improvements in the graphics. I was so engulfed in watching Brett play, it did not even occur to me to ask him if I could take a turn. I was having a great time just watching him.

We were laughing and carrying on. Brett had some difficulty doing a particular part of the game that would advance him to the next level, so he asked me if I would try. I of course said yes and played it for almost an hour. Brett was content just to watch me and told me he was fine, I could keep playing. When Yvonne came home, we did not even hear her come in the door.

We played the next day and the day after. Brett and I started going to Blockbuster Video to buy more games. They had tons of used games there for six or seven dollars each. We would buy five or six of them at a time. We couldn't wait to get home and play them. We would play all night. It wasn't long before Brett and I had become best friends. I couldn't wait for him to get home each day.

Brett really did not care what he did on the weekends. The only thing Brett wanted to do was hang around me every minute of every day. Brett was my sidekick, and I ate it up. I enjoyed coming home after work, and the minute my key went into the door, I would hear him running across the hardwood floors. He was so excited when I got home. He wanted to be the first one to greet me. I looked forward to seeing his face light up as I drove home from work every afternoon.

I did not really know how to act around him. I knew then Yvonne and I would eventually get married, and I didn't want Brett to look at me as his father. His father was a decent man, and he loved Brett. I wanted to help Brett if I could. Brett had Bipolar Disorder, and Yvonne cautioned me about this. Though years earlier, I too was diagnosed with Bipolar Disorder, I was not sure what the symptoms were, and I had no clue how this would manifest itself through a child. I did ask Yvonne some questions and read up on it. I eventually just figured I would know what to do when the time came.

Yvonne could not have been more pleased to see the relationship between us develop. She commented to me one day, I brought a completely new dynamic to the house, and Brett had never been so happy. Brett and Yvonne did not live in a neighborhood full of young kids who were Brett's age. Brett did not really have a kid to play with until I came along.

I knew I would be living there soon enough, and when this happened, I knew would be asked to do parental things for and with Brett. I never considered the role of the stepdad. After Dianne and I were divorced, I had gotten myself an apartment where I was living when Yvonne and I were dating. The lease was almost up, and Yvonne told me that she wanted me there full-time and asked me not to renew my lease. I had not yet asked Yvonne to marry me. I always said I did not ever want to be with any woman who had kids, but my relationship with Brett changed my mind. In addition to loving Yvonne, I was now very excited about being in Brett's life. I decided I would ask Yvonne to marry me, but first, I wanted to get permission.

Brett and I were out one day, and I asked him how he felt about me spending so much time at the house. He said he loved it when I came over. He said when he came home and I wasn't there, the first thing he would ask his mother was, "Where is Tom?" or "Is Tom coming over?" I explained to him how I felt about his mom, and I told him that I wanted to do a few things. I told him I wanted to hang out with him every day. I told him I wanted to live in his house with him and his mother. I explained to him in order for this to happen, I would have to marry his mother. I then asked him, "Brett, how would you feel about this?"

Brett's face lit up, and he said, "I think that would be great Tom. What should I call you?" I laughed, and told him that we would just be Tom and Brett.

Yvonne and I were together just over six months when I proposed to her. My proposal was not traditional by any means. Only a lady like Yvonne could have appreciated such a proposal. During our first months together, Yvonne had indicated to me she was in this for the long term. I was happy to hear of this. Yvonne had told me she did not want me to buy her a ring because she would most likely lose it. I heard her words and believed her, and so I did not buy her a ring for my proposal.

Yvonne and I had been driving around shopping a month prior and while we were in a music store, she really took a shine to a twelve string acoustic guitar. She almost bought it but chickened out at the last minute. I felt this would be an ample substitute for a ring. I purchased the guitar, and on the way home, I stopped at a jewelry store and asked if they had an old jewelry box I could purchase. I explained to the jeweler the situation, and he was unwilling to sell me a box because his boxes had the name of his store on them. He did however, give me a very nice, small cardboard box that the rings were shipped in. In the parking lot, I took a guitar pick and placed it carefully in the crevice where a ring would normally go.

When I got home, I asked Yvonne if she wanted to sit on the back porch and enjoy the beautiful day. She was agreeable, and as we went outside, I told her I had to use the bathroom and would be right back. I ran out to my car and got the guitar case. I set it up in the den, so Yvonne would see it when we came inside. I put the box containing the guitar pick in my pocket, got myself an iced tea and went out to sit with Yvonne.

It was not until this moment when fear came over me. It made no sense. We had talked about it, and there was no rational reason to assume she would say no. I sat with her for about an hour, and I said, "Yvonne, I have something for you."

She said, "Oh, that is nice, Tom." I reached into my pocket and pulled the box out. She was shocked, she opened it slowly and was relieved to see the guitar pick.

She smiled, and I got down on one knee and told her I loved her, and asked, "Yvonne, will you please marry me?" She was speechless. She said nothing. It was an eerie dead silence. I said, "Yvonne, my knee is killing me. I wish you would answer me, so I can sit down in my chair."

Yvonne cried and said, "Of course, I will!" She stopped crying shortly after and then commented on how thoughtful it was to get her a guitar pick, for the proposal. I said, "Oh, yeah! Come inside, Yvonne!" When we got into the house, she was pleasantly surprised to see the guitar case. She looked at me with anticipation before opening it. She very slowly opened the case, and she began to cry again. We were both so happy. Yvonne got a new guitar, and I proved to myself I could manage to do something nice for a woman and not have it result in a rash of insults where I sat in a chair and wondered why life is so difficult.

Yvonne and I were engaged for six months when she said, "Tom, I don't want a big wedding. I thought about us going to a courthouse or whatever, and afterwards we could go shopping for some kick-ass electronic toys."

I wanted to explode at that moment. If I had not already been certain she was the woman for me, this statement would have clinched it for sure. The only reason we were engaged for six months was our own procrastination. Yvonne and I are both ADHD. Certainly, someone could say our wedding was a disaster. I would say it was a fabulous disaster.

I was on a vacation from work, and I got up and got motivated to take care of the arrangements. I called a notary public, whose number I got from the internet and made an appointment for the next day for Yvonne and me to get married. She got home later and I asked if she had to work tomorrow. She said she did not have to work because she asked for Valentine's Day off. I did not realize the next day was Valentine's Day.

I told Yvonne I made our appointment to get married tomorrow at 10 a.m. She laughed and did not believe I did not know the next day was Valentine's Day. She thought it was great, and that neither of us would forget our anniversary under these circumstances. This was now my soon-to-be ADHD wife. She was not being disingenuous when she said she did not want a ring. She told me she did not want a wedding, and she really did not. I had found the perfect woman and in one day, I would have the perfect wife, but the story does not end here.

We had a 10 a.m. appointment with the notary. All I knew was the time and the address. We got up and got dressed that morning and using Yahoo maps, I printed out directions to the place we were to be married. As I followed my directions bringing us closer to our destination, I was feeling less and less encouraged about the arrangements I had made.

I parked the car at the run down strip-mall whose address matched my printed directions. I knew we were at the right place, but I hoped somehow I was wrong. I looked at Yvonne, and I said to her, "Babe, I am begging you, please wait here in the car for a moment." She agreed.

I walked into the place hoping it was not the place. There were two black men in the office having a heated discussion. One was wearing coveralls, and he was yelling at the other man who was wearing a dashiki. They were having a discussion about one's nephew, who was in jail for possession of methamphetamine. As the yelling man in coveralls left, he said to the dashiki man, "We paid you your damn money. Now, you better get him out of there." I was horrified as I watched this man leave.

As soon as the door shut, the dashiki man said to me in the most cheerful African accent, "Hello! Are you Tom Nardone?" I swear to God, I said, "I am not sure, let me go find out."

I went out to the car, and Yvonne asked, "What's the deal, Tom?"

I said, "Yvonne, you have two choices, and I will leave this up to you. I am good either way. We can either postpone our wedding for another day, or we can have a kick-ass story how we got married on Valentine's Day, at a bail bondsman's office."

Yvonne looked at me and smiled. She said, "Tom, I want you, but I definitely want the kick-ass story, too."

We got married, and it only cost us fifteen dollars. We went straight to the electronics store afterwards.

Life, as I know it today, had begun.

Things were going to be a little different from now on between Brett and me. I was now "The Dad". Yvonne had been the primary disciplinarian prior to my arrival. I knew it was best for one person to make decisions regarding Brett and his behavior problems, and I asked Yvonne if I could take care of this. She felt Brett and I had become close, and I would do a good job with him.

I explained this to Brett, and he was naïvely excited about it. A few people told me Brett was bipolar, therefore would not be able to do certain things as a result. I was told by teachers and others he would not go to college or even graduate from high school. I chose not to believe them. I saw what Brett was capable of, and I knew he would be able to do whatever he wanted to do.

I was ADHD, and I knew nothing about being a father. I did however volunteer for the role as disciplinarian. I suppose I saw Brett with the challenges he was having and saw myself in him and wanted to help. I saw a kid who was having trouble in school and had no friends. I was thrilled about the opportunity to teach him what I had to learn the hard way. The other reason I took this on was my father. My father had been gone for a few years, but I still remembered what he taught me. When the time came for me to assume my role as stepdad, I really thought I was ready.

It wasn't long until I was no longer sure I had what it took to be a stepdad. I began to think I was doing well to manage my own life. I did not know how in the hell I was going to manage someone else's life on top of it. It had just registered to me: I was now responsible for the success of a nine-year-old, and I was his role model.

I was scared and considered asking Yvonne to take back control. It later occurred to me: This is not about me. Brett needed me. The way in which he was being disciplined had not been very successful thus far. I do not blame or judge anyone for it, but the truth was Brett had incredible problems behaving at school and doing his work.

I loved Brett and decided I would act like I loved him. I decided I would believe in myself the same way I would expect him to believe in himself. I would use the same playbook my father used with me. I believed it would work because I saw much of myself in Brett. As it turned out, Brett really did need me, but I needed him, too. I just decided I was going to dad-up.

Yvonne was an extraordinarily good mother. She loved Brett unconditionally. Yvonne was good with Brett when things were calm and there was no drama, but Yvonne was also a little bit country, where I was a little bit Rock 'n' Roll.

Chapter 15

The first time I had to deal with Brett was very shortly after I explained to him he would now be answering to me. He came home from his dad's house on a Saturday afternoon. He had a school assignment due the following Monday, and he asked his mother on Friday if he could do it Saturday afternoon, instead of the moment he got home from school. Yvonne told him he could wait, and they agreed to this.

Saturday morning before Brett got home, I told Yvonne I was going to buy some parts for a computer I was going to build. I asked where Brett was because I wanted him to come with me. Yvonne told me he would be home in a few minutes, but he had to work on his homework before he went anywhere. I told her I would wait for him to do his work and take him with me because I loved going places with Brett.

Brett came in the door and said hello to Yvonne and me. Yvonne asked if he had a good time at his dad's, and he said he did. She then told him, he would need to go ahead and get started on his homework. Brett began to cry and whine about it. Yvonne made this arrangement with Brett prior to my appointment as disciplinarian, so she wanted to deal with this issue. I just observed.

Yvonne explained to him when he was finished, I was going to take him with me to go to the computer store. Brett did not care, he just did not want to do the homework. They went back and forth for ten minutes as Yvonne continually tried to reason with him. This whole exchange made absolutely no sense to me, and I could see nothing Yvonne was saying was going to get his attention.

I got up and said, "Screw this! I am just going by myself. I don't need this kind of drama on my day off." I started up the stairs to get my wallet and my keys. Brett immediately stopped crying and ran up the stairs after me.

He said, "Tom, Tom, Tom! Okay, okay, I will do it. I will do my work, and then we can go, okay?"

I said in a very calm and soft-spoken voice, "Did you hear me say I was going by myself?"

He said, "Yes, but I want to go with you."

I laughed and asked Brett, still with a very soft-spoken voice, "Brett, are you trying to negotiate with me?"

He asked, "What is that?"

I explained to him what it was so I was sure he understood, and again, in a very soft-spoken voice, I asked him. "Are you trying to negotiate with me?"

Brett said proudly, "Yes, I want to negotiate."

Brett moved closer to me because I spoke in a softer voice as I said to him, "Brett, I am the boss around here from now on, so there is something you should know about me."

Brett asked, "What is that, Tom?"

I then said, this time at the top of my lungs and as loud as I could shout, "I don't negotiate! I talk, and you fly! Now! Go downstairs and get your homework immediately!"

Brett was down those stairs before the echo of my yelling ended. I left and when I got back, Brett was watching TV with his mother. I asked Brett if his homework was done, and he said "Yes, and mom checked it, Tom. Can I help you build your computer?"

I said, "Sure you can. Come on up with me."

I did not want to yell at Brett. He depended on his pouting and crying to carry the day as it always had before. He had used this as currency in the past and was usually successful. The bank of Tom Nardone had never accepted this type of currency nor would it ever.

I was not about to see him emerge victorious after such a display of disrespect toward his mother. I knew I could never back down on anything I ever told Brett I would do. I saw much of myself in him, and I just decided I would do things the way my father did them. I did question my tactics from time to time, but I had to believe he would respect me, the way I respected my own father.

Table manners were a problem as well. Brett, once showed me how unlearned he was in the importance of behaving at the dinner table. Yvonne and I were off one Saturday. I hung out with Brett while she worked her fingers to the bone creating an exquisite meal for dinner. The dinner was to be four or five courses, and she planned it all very carefully. She worked most of the day on it. She asked me not to eat too much because of the feast she had planned. When the three of us sat down, she already had the table set. After all her hard work, she could finally sit down to rest and enjoy the fruits of her labor.

Brett had been a little wound up, and I had a few minor occurrences with him, but we made it to the dinner table without a major incident.

Yvonne had really outdone herself. The table and the presentation of the food was a culinary masterpiece. Things began great, and we were laughing and talking and having a delightful time. Until halfway through dinner, I noticed Brett looking around as if trying to make a decision.

I took note of this immediately. He then leaned over to one side. I said to myself, "Oh, no." As soon as he got himself positioned, he cranked out a fart that was as loud as a chainsaw. He was able to sustain this fart for such a long time I actually sat there and waited for it to end.

Yvonne just gave a defeated sigh and began to get up and leave the table. I put my hand on her arm and said in a gentle voice "No, Babe. Sit down, I got this." It was time once again for me to get into character. I looked over at Brett who was still laughing, and with a single facial expression from me, his gastric bliss turned to piss as I watched his happiness fade from his face. It was then when I realized had the power of "The Look".

I calmly said, "Brett, stand up please." He did so. I then said, "Brett, pick up your plate and your drink." He did so. I then slid open the patio door and said, "Brett, go on outside and finish your dinner." It was raining and very cold. He thought I might be joking. I told him as I pointed at my own face, "Brett, do you see this? This is my no nonsense face. That means I am not kidding, so for the last time, bring your plate, your cup and your ass out onto the patio under the roof. Animals eat outside. You are an animal. You will eat outside." Yvonne and I had a delightful time as we finished the meal on which she worked so tirelessly. Brett finished, and he went straight to bed.

The next morning Brett came down to eat breakfast. I was already up. He said cheerfully, "Good morning, Tom."

I said, "Good morning, Brett." He poured himself a bowl of cereal and then sat down at the table. I said, "Brett, you seem to be unclear on something. Your training on how to live among human beings is unfortunately ongoing." He couldn't believe it.

He said, "Well, then I just won't eat then."

I said in a tone as if I were talking to a two-year-old, "Oh Brett... that is so cute. You think I am your mother, and you are implementing a hunger strike." I changed my voice back to the no nonsense mode and continued, "Here is the thing, Brett. I don't have any requirement of you to eat. I do, however, have a requirement that if you do eat, you will be doing so outdoors with the rest of the animals for which manners don't apply."

He said, "I don't appreciate you calling me an animal, Tom."

I said, "Fortunately for you, Brett, your gratitude is also not required." For three days, he ate outside, and to this day, table manners are among his most-honed skill sets.

I was sovereign. This fact was true of my father, and it was true of me. Brett would go to his mother with things he knew I would not have a favorable answer to. He would make these deals with her, and it would always end in tragedy. Brett promised his mom that he would clean his shit-pit of a room on Saturday afternoon. He chose this time because he knew I would be at work. He figured if I was not there, he would be able to avoid it.

When the time came, Brett defied his mother and refused to clean his room. Yvonne rarely called me at work over such matters, and she would only do so after her own diplomatic attempts had failed or as a last resort. When I got the call, I was in my boss' office, and she will never forget this.

My boss and I were joking around, and I heard the page I had a phone call. It was about an hour before I was to go home for the day. Yvonne explained the situation. I said to Yvonne in a slow, anxious and almost evil whisper, "Put... Him... On!"

I looked at my boss and said, "Excuse me, Andrea, I have to get into character for a moment." She of course had no idea what I meant. While I waited for Brett to pick up, I pulled the office door shut, and there was a silence.

Brett, in a very humble and nervous voice said, "Hello?"

Following Brett's *Hello*, I shouted at full volume, as if I were Kurt Russell in *Tombstone*, "Well, you called down the thunder, and now you got it, mister! Your mother told you to get your room clean, and that's not good enough for you? Well, now I'm coming, and hell's coming with me, you hear? Hell's coming with me!" I hung up the phone, and said to my boss, "Okay, I'm back." She looked at me as if I were insane.

With only those words, I fixed everything at home, and I did it over the telephone. Everything in Brett's life made sense at the end of our brief conversation. The reason for this was an important thing that happened when I said those words. I got something from Brett others were not able or willing to get from him. I got his attention. If we examine what happened, there are some important points to note.

I did not tell Brett to go clean his room. I did not tell Brett to listen to his mother, and I did not tell Brett to be cutting the grass as I pulled into the driveway only one hour after our conversation ended. I did not tell him to do anything, but when I got home he had listened to his mother, cleaned his room and yes, he was cutting the front lawn as I pulled into the driveway.

Just as my father did for me, I got Brett's attention. Brett was in his own little world, and he thought this was the world in which he lived, for a moment. I was kind enough to tell him this was a world he can only fantasize about. He lived in my world. Teaching Brett how to behave on Planet Tom was not quickly accomplished. It was not a race; it was a marathon.

I do not know what my father's solution would have been for everything. Brett was constantly being disrespectful to his mom, my wife. Dad and I never had this conversation. I never said a disrespectful thing to my mother as a child. Yvonne was such a sweet lady she never began with an assertive tone. She always gave Brett every chance to keep the peace. Occasionally, it worked, but it would often end up with Brett being insensitive or disrespectful. This angered me to tears to see. This and his grades were the biggest source of trouble for Brett.

Many times, Brett was unaware his words or his actions were rude or hurtful. There were not any kids his age in our neighborhood, and he was with mostly behaviorally-challenged kids at school. Brett's BD on top of it made things difficult. I knew Brett, and I did not punish him for every little thing he did wrong. I would always listen to his side of the story. I tried to always give him the benefit of the doubt. If I felt he was not intentionally hurtful, I would simply have a civil discussion with him.

The constant back-talking his mother, pretending not to hear her or just not listening to her. All of those things bothered me, but sometimes, Yvonne and I would plan a movie or something for the family to do. I would then go to ask Brett if he wanted to come along with us. He would say, "Can't it just be me and you, Tom?"

Brett loved his mother, and she knew this, but it was still difficult for her to hear her son ask to exclude her. I hated this more than anything he did. I knew he did not necessarily have a problem with being around his mother, and I knew he just enjoyed the camaraderie of he and I being out and doing things together.

I politely explained to him each time, but I could no longer watch Yvonne get her feelings hurt. For over two years, I could not get him to understand, but I was determined to put a stop to this. I would have never yelled at or punished Brett for this. I could see other people had influenced Brett's behavior, and he learned to behave this way. I knew I would have to try something a little different. Perhaps, I could let him see an example of how it feels, and he would learn firsthand how awful this was.

Yvonne and I were out running around, and I decided to pull into a local fun park. Yvonne said, "What are you doing, Tom? Brett is not here." This was Brett's favorite place to go. The next day was Sunday, and Brett would be back from his dad's house.

I said, "C'mon, Yvonne. We will have fun. I promise." She went along with me, and we had a great time. We played games, rode the go-carts and played their miniature bowling game. We really had a great time together. It was a great activity for us to do.

I knew this was Brett's favorite place, and I chose it for that reason. Sure, I wanted to have fun with my wife, but I went there for Brett's benefit. I made sure I didn't use all my tokens. I also made sure to keep a bunch of my ski ball tickets I'd won. I ordered a soft drink and was sure to hold on to the cup with the name of the place on it.

Sunday night Yvonne went to bed, and shortly thereafter, Brett came home from his dad's house. He came running up the stairs to see if I was in my man cave as he did every time he came home. I was counting on this. He came in to say hello. He immediately noticed the ski ball tickets, the tokens and the cup I had placed in my room so he was sure to see them. Brett had begun to ask me how my day was but stopped when he saw the items on display.

Brett was very upset, and said, "Tom! You and Mom went to the game place without me?"

I replied, "We sure did, and we had a great time, too, Brett. Thanks for asking. What did you and your dad do?"

Brett ignored my question and said this time a little angrier, "Why didn't you wait until I was here and take me with you?"

What I said next was not easy to say to Brett, but I had to do it. I told Brett, "Your mom suggested that, but I wanted it to be just us. I thought it would be better if it was just your mom and me without you there."

Without another word, Brett lowered his head, and with a sad face, he slowly walked out of the room as he began to cry.

This was my finest hour, and for a moment, I hated myself. As soon as the door shut, I began to cry. It killed me to say what I said to that little boy. He was my son. He was my beautiful little boy, and I knew my words would crush him. Knowing this and seeing this were not the same.

I cried harder over this than anything I ever experienced. The level at which I cried about this physically hurt, and I was in very intense pain over it. I worried it would not stop. I cannot think of anything in my life ever feeling as bad as the moments following Brett walking out of my room with his head down and in tears. I put those tears in his eyes and as unbearable as it was, I would do it again. I knew this would not be easy beforehand but did not hesitate when making this decision.

While I am not particularly proud of this story, I will stand by it. I mention it because it is important to understand: not all kids learn the same way. There are some you can reason with, and there are some you can talk to. Many ADHD kids cannot pay attention to a level where retention sets in. I was such a child, and so was Brett. Brett was without certain social skills he needed, and this was not through any fault of his own. I needed to make him understand, and this was the only way.

I made a decision to help my son understand the value of treating other people right. I wanted to teach him how the words a person says can pierce the heart of those who love them. I could not allow Brett to not understand the pain he was causing his sweet mother. I could not abide Brett being like those people I grew up with.

I put myself through this, too. I did it so Brett could understand something no one had ever been able to make him understand. Brett did not comprehend his words could destroy. I cannot imagine how he would have turned out if I did not teach him empathy. The only way I could make him understand this was to illustrate it to him. I gave his exact words back to him and made him see the pain they caused. It was an awful thing for him to see, but I offer no apology.

I originally had planned to let him stew all night, but Brett was only eleven years old, and I couldn't let him stay in his room all night, thinking that I didn't love him. I calmed down, and twenty minutes after he left my room, I went to Brett's door and gently knocked, much the same way my father knocked at my door years before.

163

In the same calm almost whispering voice my father used with me, I asked Brett if he was upset. He nodded his head. I asked him if he ever thought his mother felt like this when he said the same thing in front of her. Brett began crying, and he nodded his head even harder. I put my arm around him, and I told him I loved him. I told him he was my best friend in the whole world. We talked for a while, and I asked him if he wanted to come into my room and watch a movie with me. He said he did, and we hung out in my room watching movies until he fell asleep.

Growing up ADHD, I never did anything unless I wanted to do it or was forced to do it. I had so many problems with Brett, and I did not want to deal with any of them. I learned over the years that followed, being a parent is very hard work. Being a parent seldom involved doing what I wanted to do. It was never about what I wanted. It was about what Brett needed.

Brett literally spent the majority of the next few years on restriction or in some kind of trouble. He made things very hard for himself, and he fought it for as long as he could. By the end of his tenth grade year, he got things figured out, and he became a man.

In spite of Brett's bipolar disorder, bad grades, behavior problems, suspensions, summer school and being grounded for the majority of these years, Brett managed to do what many said he would not ever do and what he himself doubted often he would ever do.

June 15, 2013, was the proudest day of my life. I watched Brett Alexander Fuller walk across the stage at his high school graduation ceremony and receive his diploma. I can honestly say that he did this, not me. In my entire life, I have never been involved in anything so awful or so beautiful. Brett graduated from high school and became a man. I am aware of the part I played in this, but I have a tough time hearing people credit me for something I simply did not feel I had a choice with. I never thought about quitting on him; it simply was not an option.

Brett is and always will be my very best friend. Brett knows today that it was not easy for me to do what I had to do, and he understands why I did. He also understands I did them with my own personal challenges.

He has no resentment. He knows the easiest thing in the world for me to have done was to have done nothing. He has thanked me for not doing so. Today, Brett is a bright young man, with the charm of James Bond. He has a job and a car, and he is starting college in a couple of weeks. He frequently takes his mother out to the movies or to dinner. Of all my friends, there is none more thoughtful than he is. Brett Fuller is my friend, my son and my hero.

Both Yvonne and Brett gave me that which I never would have had without them. I experienced what it was to be a father. Before they came into my life, I had just accepted the fact, I would spend my life wondering about what kind of father I would have been or could have been. I would never have known if I had what it took to be a father. I would never have known how my own father felt when he had to yell at me.

I learned more about my own father from Brett than from the sum of my own experiences. I knew all the whats, but I did not know any of the whys. This is what I learned as a result of Yvonne and Brett being in my life. They helped me understand and know better the most amazing man I have ever known; my own father. Yvonne, Brett and I have weathered many storms. They both are, and ever shall be, more than just my family. They are my heart, and they are my world.
Without them, I would not know how to live.

Chapter 16

My ADHD still presents problems to me as an adult. There are many areas where I do not do as I ought to do, but Yvonne is quite understanding about my shortcomings. I acknowledge Yvonne as the boss, and when she speaks, I generally follow command. I trust her completely, and I don't typically argue with her when it comes to the business or logistics of the way our home is run. She is usually right, but sometimes it takes a moment for me to realize this.

It was three months after we were married, I came home from work in a particularly good mood. When I entered our bedroom, Yvonne was busy cleaning. She was gathering up all of my things, and she informed me that my man-cave was now far more than just a man-cave. It was now to be my bedroom. Her reasons were simply that I was messy, and she did not want to share a bathroom with me. Yvonne was not as comfortable living in filth as I was.

I was outraged. I told her this was crazy and asked her, "Hey, what the hell kind of marriage is this any way if we don't even sleep in the same bed?" She stuck to her guns and did not waver. I cowered off to regroup, and I thought I would come back at her later when I had gathered some more talking points. I changed my mind and decided not to go back, and I just played along because I figured she was just on her cycle or something. I did not want to stir the beehive any further.

I was sitting in my room pouting and feeling like a loser. After ten or fifteen minutes, I tried to maybe put a positive spin on my excommunication. I began thinking of all the things that might be beneficial as a result of my solitude. As I ran down the list of positives, I began to realize that there was really was no downside. I watch what I want to watch on the TV. I play video games all night long if I so chose. I didn't even have to worry about waking her. We already decided when I moved in I could be in charge of my man-cave. This means no one telling me to pick up after myself. I was now the Lord and Master of my very own skid row.

Then, I started worrying about something else. I began worrying that she might want to switch back. She might come to her "senses" and decide a husband and wife should live in the same bedroom. This would be the end of my kingdom.

As it turned out this became permanent, and the two of us were never happier. I enjoy waking up and seeing Yvonne sitting on the sofa wide awake as she is belting out "Sweet Home Alabama" on her ukulele. I can say good morning to her, and she is glad to see me. She will say, "Hey, Tom, how did you sleep?"

To which I reply, "Great, dear!"

The alternative could go something like this:

Yvonne wakes up and with a bed head says, "Tom you kept me up all night, and I could not sleep. You need to get your stuff picked up today before you do anything else. I can't live like this." Then, I tell her I will get to it and never even think about it.

No sir. I prefer to leave my squalor upstairs and enter my living room to the sound of a singing wife.

My biggest challenge with ADHD has always been my getting irritated at the simplest things in life. My medication keeps my irritability at bay for the most part, but medication or not, I cannot seem to be comfortable anywhere on earth except in my own house. I cannot stand to be away from it unnecessarily. I go to work five days a week, and every now and then, I go to a rock concert, but that is it.

I don't know what irritates me more; leaving the house or knowing I will be leaving the house to go somewhere in the near future. The appointed time and place loom over me like a black cloud of frustration, and I can't think about anything else until it is over.

The idea of being anywhere else causes me tremendous anxiety. I am unable to focus on anything except how long will it be until we are home. One of the reasons is I worry someone will break in while we are gone. We actually have an old car in the driveway we haven't driven in four years. Yvonne wanted to sell it, but I insisted it stay parked in the driveway to keep away the burglars.

Fear of burglars is only one of many reasons I am uncomfortable away from home. There are other reasons, and I have no problem admitting the biggest one. I am a lazy son-of-a-bitch.

Yvonne has honed her craft, and she has become better at getting me out of the house. In the morning after I come down, I get a cup of coffee and go directly to my chair. Yvonne will wait a few minutes and bring my medication to me and hand me a glass of water. She waits about twenty minutes and then ever so carefully segues into her plans for the day.

There is actually only one thing worse than being away from the house. It is the guilt I feel when Yvonne wants to do something with me, and I refuse. I cannot bear to see my wife sad or upset. I would rather die than disappoint my wife. If Yvonne is hell-bent on doing something I will almost always agree do it with her. Otherwise what good am I?

Yvonne and I used to go grocery shopping together, but Yvonne couldn't take my constant whining. She forbade me to go with her ever again. The idea of her performing brain surgery on herself seems less of a chore.

When I went grocery shopping with her, I found it to be excruciating. I walked up and down the aisles with her thinking only *Is this the last aisle?* The biggest problem was I cannot stand to be asked the same question over and over. She asked me, "Tom, will you eat this?" and she asked me several times on each aisle. No matter how many times I said, "Yvonne, I have no preference. It is all just fuel to me anyway," she insisted on asking. I know she did this because she cares about me, but that did not make it any easier.

I don't know what it was about grocery shopping, but I felt like I was going to lose it. Unable to fight the urge, I asked Yvonne, "How much longer is this going to go on?" I offered to eat nothing but peanut butter sandwiches to save time and money, and she just looked at me as if I were crazy.

I didn't just try to make the shopping end prematurely. I was proactive in extending the time between grocery store visits. I would actually eat less just so I could have more time in between trips to the store. I even suggested things for dinner or I cooked just to create the illusion we had lots of food in the house. Sooner or later, the day always came.

The last time we went grocery shopping, I definitely went too far.

We were in the grocery store, and I was whining as I always did, and Yvonne kept telling me to stop. She was never mean about telling me this, and she usually managed to have a sense of humor about it. I was in rare form this day, and the urge to cry about being at the grocery store was at full power. We had an entire cart of groceries, and my concern was we had already been there for a long time. The longer we were at the store, the more groceries we buy. The more groceries we buy, the longer it takes to check out. Then, there is loading them, unloading them and putting them away. I felt I had to do something to salvage my day.

Yvonne had taken about as much of my whining as she could take for one day. I said, "Yvonne, we have already been on this aisle twice. We have enough food. When are we getting the hell out of here? Why does my day off have to turn into some kind of an endurance test?"

To which she replied, "We are finished right now!" I heard no humor in her tone.

She let go of the cart and began storming out of the store toward the exit. All I could think of was that we had already wasted so much time, and now we would have to repeat it at some point very soon. I tried to tell her I would behave and let's go back in the store and get our groceries. Yvonne would not speak to me the whole way home except when she said, "If I hear you say one more word, I will stop this car, park it in the middle of the street, get out and walk back to the house!" I did not say another word.

When we got home, she went to her bedroom and slammed the door. I quietly went up to my man-cave and closed the door very gently and sat on my futon, not knowing exactly what I should do. I figured I didn't want to be doing anything too fun in case she came up to talk to me. I could not take the suspense any longer. I thought I would make an unbelievable gesture of goodwill. I decided to go down there and offer to go back to the grocery store and do the shopping myself. This was to be my way of apologizing.

When I got to her room, I told her I wanted to tell her something, but she asked if she could speak first. I agreed. She said, "Tom, I know how you are about the grocery shopping and the questions. Look, from now on you are never coming grocery shopping with me. I can't take the bullshit from you while I am trying to plan meals." She then explained all I had to do was to clean the kitchen while she was gone and bring the groceries inside when she came home. After she spoke, I was speechless. It finally ended. I was free from yet another shackle in my life.

When Yvonne asked what I wanted to say, I just said, "Oh, nothing."

Being ADHD I am prone to being impulsive. This does not happen often, but when it does, it always seems to bring a consequence. Yvonne finds this to be attractive. She refers to it as a child-like excitement. When I get excited, I am just like a child. I even think like a child when

169

I get excited. It happens so quickly, I don't take time to look at the big picture. It is usually an impulsive idea that causes this. I think only of what we are going to do, and I give very little thought to details of the preparation or consequences.

This doesn't just happen with Yvonne. This mostly happens when Brett and I are left alone in the house without any adult supervision. Brett and I can be very impulsive when we are together.

Once, Yvonne returned from the grocery store, and as was her wish, she came home to a clean kitchen and an empty trash can. I brought the groceries into the house, and she began putting them away. She was in a fantastic mood. When she got finished putting the groceries away, she asked if I wanted to make up some hamburgers and put them on the grill while she was in the bathtub. She also inquired if I wanted to watch a movie while we ate. I said, "Sure that would be great!"

Before she left she said, "Okay, there is a pack of ground beef on the counter."

I went into the kitchen and noticed that she bought a giant six-pound pack of hamburger meat. I thought it was little excessive to buy six pounds of hamburger meat for the two of us to have hamburgers, but I figured we could eat the rest of them the next day. I lit the grill, and proceeded to make the hamburger up into patties. I went outside and put all nineteen of them on the grill. When the hamburgers were finished I put them on a large serving plate and went inside.

Apparently, Yvonne had not intended for all six pounds of hamburger to be used for hamburgers. She bought it because she had planned out dinners for the week and much of what she bought was for the purpose of making meals. This had not occurred to me at the time. She thought I would have the foresight to put a large portion of the ground beef in the refrigerator or the freezer.

Moments after I came inside, Yvonne entered the kitchen, and hell followed her. She saw me standing there with a giant plate of nineteen hamburgers, and a big smile on my face. When I saw her expression, I knew there was something wrong. I knew it was about to get gangster up in my house. Yvonne looked at me in disbelief. She could not talk for a few seconds, and admittedly I was scared. She finally shouted, "Tom! Are you crazy?"

I said, "What's the matter, darlin'?"

Yvonne responded, "I did not buy six pounds of ground beef for us to have one meal today!"

I said angrily, "Hey, calm down it's only Friday. We will have every one of these eaten before the weekend is over."

Yvonne was still furious. She said, "Well, I don't want to watch a movie now, and I have lost my appetite! Enjoy your hamburgers." She stormed off to her bedroom, and she would have calmed down if I had just kept my mouth shut, but my feelings were hurt.

"Well, now I am not hungry. You have upset me, and now I can't eat. I will just put them in the refrigerator."

Yvonne, after hearing this, came storming back into the kitchen and snatched the plate of nineteen hamburgers out of my hand, and threw them in the trash can. She put the empty plate back into my hand, and stormed off again. She got half way down the hall and came back. I looked in the trash, and then I heard her coming back. When she got back she pushed me out of the way and took the bag with the nineteen hamburgers out of the can. She then emptied the cat's litter box into the bag and took it into the garage and put it into the garbage can.

She came back, and I was still standing there with an empty plate in one hand and a spatula in the other. She said, "I knew you would just eat them out of the garbage can, so I emptied the litter box into the bag. Don't bother going out there looking at them because I shook the bag before I put it in the can!" Then, she went to her room and slammed the door. This whole drama lasted about two minutes from the time I entered to the time the door slammed.

I quietly put the plate and the spatula in the sink and went upstairs to my room. I sat there and began reviewing the events. I thought about it from her point of view, and while I thought she overreacted, I suppose she did spend a lot of time and planning. I determined that she had a right to be upset. A couple of hours later, she came up to my room as I was sure she would and apologized to me. I forgave her, and we watched the movie.

Brett and I were hanging out one weekend alone, as Yvonne was sick in her bed. It was the fourth of July, and Brett went up to the fireworks stand and bought a bunch of fireworks. Yvonne was furious because he was not allowed to shoot fireworks. I told her I would supervise him, and she told me I was not allowed to shoot off fireworks. We argued, and she caved.

Brett and I were out there for a while in broad daylight shooting of fireworks because we could not wait until it was dark outside. We were at it for about twenty minutes. We shot half of them off, got bored and quit for the day. We went inside and watched movies until we went to bed that night.

The next morning Brett wanted to shoot the rest of the fireworks off. I agreed. We shot one or two off, and we got bored. I asked Brett if he had any old toys he wanted to blow up, but he didn't. He and I went into the garage looking for something to destroy with the fireworks. I found an old plastic bag. I pulled an old pot out of it and said, "Let's see what it does to this."

We went back to the backyard, and I carefully placed a firework shell under the pot. I told Brett to get back, and I lit in and ran. It blew up and spread fire all over the backyard and in the wooded area beyond the fence. Brett and I began stomping them out. When we finished we went back to look at the pot, and the shell had actually torn the pot in half. We were laughing so hard, we had tears. I foolishly thought Yvonne would find this as funny as we did. I was wrong.

When I entered Yvonne's room, I was holding the pot behind my back and laughing. I did not realize she was asleep. I woke her with my laughter. She asked, "What are you waking me up for?" Having no brain, I told her what we did and showed her the pot. She looked at me as if I destroyed a car. She lost it. I did not really expect all the yelling. Apparently, these pots are a little hard to come by, and she searched everywhere for them and found them at Goodwill.

I explained to her what I thought was relevant information. I said, "The pot was in a garbage bag and has been sitting in the garage for over a year. You haven't even taken it in the house." She asked me if something that belonged to me is in in the garage and has been there for over a year, could she destroy it for the sheer fun of it. It was not until this moment I understood the wrong in what I had done. Like the nineteen hamburgers, it really made sense to me at that moment, but it was too late. The pot was worthless.

I was hungry and excited about watching a movie, and I acted without thinking. I impulsively made nineteen hamburgers, and it just never occurred to me there might be a reason for the size of the package. I was excited about blowing things up with the fireworks, and I did not consider Yvonne still wanted a pot that had been in the garage for a year. I was just as excited as I had been watching the red kite on the T-ball field.

Yvonne gets over things quickly, and she does not allow me to feel prolonged periods of guilt. She eventually realizes that our relationship is bigger than a pot or six pounds of meat. Yvonne describes me as hot or cold with no in between. There are only two speeds with me; stop and go. I am obsessive about the things that interest me, and I want nothing to do with the things that don't interest me. I can't just have a thing I am interested in a little bit. It is all or nothing. I become obsessed with things very easily. It is this obsessiveness that led to me becoming a writer.

My life was such that I would go to work, come home, spend a little time with the family and then retire to my man-cave and play games until bedtime. Yvonne was getting a little annoyed with me because I was spending so much time playing. She said I was as an obsessed child, and she was right.

I scheduled days off from work around the release days of some of these video games. I would be at the game store at midnight, with the rest of the kids, waiting to pick my game up the moment it was available. When this one particular game came out, she found out I went on vacation to have a whole week to play it. When I began playing this game, I did not shower or come downstairs for six days, and she could hold her tongue no longer.

She said, "Tom, I am not going to tell you what to do, but can you not think of something more productive to do with your time off?" Out of love for Yvonne, I thought about it. I thought I would look at some career opportunities and put my game controller down for a little while.

I thought maybe I would teach myself computer programming. I thought maybe I could get a better job and improve my life a bit. I bought a couple of books, and I wanted to see if maybe I could start out learning PHP and C++.

I wrote some sample codes, but I needed a website to test them. I got a website and wrote an article called, "The Theory of Pants". I needed some people to read it and leave a comment, so I could see if my code worked. A few people read it, and they really loved it. They thought it was funny and told me so. I wrote another and then another, and I was really enjoying myself.

I did not enjoy learning how to write computer code, but these stories of mine were starting to get traction in the blogging community. I decided it was more important for me to entertain the world than to educate myself or have a better job. I shit-canned the notion of being a computer programmer and decided to keep writing. I had become a blogger before even knowing what a blog was.

I also began reading other people and began building a following. All of my articles were just my own observations of the world and my opinions about various parts of it. I would test them out on my wife, and she would read them and look at me funny and say, "Tom, Baby, what are you doing?" She could not understand why I was so willing to share embarrassing moments from my life with the world. I just thought what I had to say was funny. I like entertaining people, but the attention I was now getting was overwhelming.

I never ever wanted or desired to be a writer. It was not a lifelong dream of mine. The idea of it had never even occurred to me. Writing came very easy for me. I am not as much of an extrovert as people think I am. I am actually very introverted. I find it very difficult to walk up to people and introduce myself. The blog is a great way to avoid this. It was easy to write something and send it out blindly to complete strangers. Through my blog I have become a character that I happen to play in real life.

One day, while trying to decide what to write about, I chose to write about my ADHD. My first ADHD article was called ADHD is awesome. It did pretty well. Later, I published the story you read about the kid peeing on my shoe in the first grade. This story went nuts, and so I decided to start a new blog devoted only to ADHD, and so adhdpeople.net was born.

Were it not for my wife asking me to find something more productive to do, and asking in a nice way, it may not have ever happened. Thank you, Yvonne.

Conclusion

I have spent the majority of my life living in a world that did not understand or appreciate me. The majority of my school career was spent trying to be accepted by those who were considered "normal". At most of my jobs, I worked for people who could not appreciate me which resulted in rejection in the form of termination. My own wife for years did not accept the fact I was not like everyone else. I was nothing but a disappointment to her, and she never gave me a break. Her rejection, while it was well-received, was in the form of a divorce.

A large part of my life was a life of being rejected by people I desperately wanted to be accepted by. I spent a great deal of time trying to be the person others wanted me to be. I worked so hard at trying to fit in and being the way normal people were only to fail time after time. As I reviewed my life in writing about these things, it occurred to me. The toughest things in my life stopped being a problem when I stopped caring about them. It was easy to quit caring about them since I had no hope or belief they would ever change. What I discovered was the person I was, was a kick-ass human being whose awesomeness had no limits.

I spent the majority of my time in school feeling the constant rejection from students and teachers. In my first marriage, I spent the majority of it worrying daily about every little thing I did that might disappoint my wife. I was so afraid of being alone, I married her and let her lead me around by the nose.

I hoped the students would change. I hoped the teachers would change. I hoped my wife would change. I wasted so much time waiting for the problem to go away. I did not know then what the problem was. I thought the problem was the people who did not accept me.

The problem was me. It was I who constantly put pressure on myself. It was I who wanted to be liked by others. It was I who let my need to be accepted consume me, my grades and my life. It was who I made all of this the priority. Ultimately, it was I who fixed it when I just stopped giving a shit.

Trying to be someone else is exhausting. There is no difference today between the person I am and the person I want to be. I do not factor in the expectations of others when making life decisions. For me, the key was to like myself and be myself. I never found peace until I did this. Today, when I meet people, they get a pure unabridged version of Tom Nardone. They can like me, or they cannot like me. I am good either way. I believe this attitude is a result of my experiences.

I do not excuse or forgive the people who wronged me. I don't care enough about them to hate them any longer. I would not change anything about my life. It has brought me to the place I am, and I am grateful for the person I became. I suppose something good came from it in the end. I can't say everything resulting from my youth is helpful to me today. I am certainly not without my issues.

Today, when look back to the beginning, when I see the picture of me as a child in the first grade, I see that little boy as a person other than myself. I have the memories, and I know I am the boy in the photo, but I see him as a different person than the person I have become. He was innocent. He was kind. He was polite, considerate and curious. Inside of him, there was no hate or malice. All he wanted was to make friends and to make his father and mother proud of him. He had no anger in him. He was beautiful.

There is much hate in me today. I don't think about all the people who have wronged me or treated me poorly, but when I do, I find myself unable to forgive them. I am not interested in knowing them, and I don't think today any of them are aware of the profound impact their actions had on my life.

Today, I am Tom Nardone, and I am ADHD. In spite of my "disorder" I have become awesome. I consider myself to be a success. I realize a large portion of what you have read was the many ways in which I felt like the world was against me. I did not write it to muster sympathy. I don't want anybody to feel bad for me. The point, I suppose, is I never gave up on myself. Though many times, I wanted to just that. I stayed the course and today, I am all I ever wanted to be, and all my father ever wanted me to be. I am happy. Being Tom Nardone is awesome, and I am never going to try to be anyone else.

I am not a CEO sitting on top of a pile of cash telling you my stories of global conquest in the business world. I am not an athlete who worked every day with his goals clearly in front of him and who didn't stop until an Olympic gold medal was placed around his neck. I am not even a guy who figured out some secret to happiness. Today, I am just hoping to hold on to my job in the hopes my wife and I can continue making the mortgage payments, so we can keep our house. I am nobody special.

There was a time when my life was going nowhere. There was a time when I definitely considered my ADHD a disorder. I do not consider it such today. Without treatment, I would not have made it. My treatment was the single most important thing to which I attribute my success. Almost nothing in my adult life worked out until the day I made the decision to be treated.

For me, it was medication. As an ADHD adult who is treated, I can tell you how many problems vanished after treatment; the answer is zero. I am able to manage these problems better as a result of my medication. There is no cure for ADHD, and I would not want there to be. I have never felt the need to hide my ADHD. I believe it is a part of me, and I love myself. It beats the hell out of being ordinary.

I love the people I have met in the ADHD community. The ADHD community is very small in comparison to many other groups of people. We do not have hundreds of people actively lobbying congress for money. We do not have a large parade where we stick it in people's faces and try to make them like it or accept it.

We are a group of people who spent most of our lives unaware we had this "disorder". Those of us who are vocal or have a need to speak about it do so predominantly on social media networks. We simply are a community who understand each other. The ADHD people I know have a great empathy for others with the same difficulties. I see every day as people come together to help each other freely online for the purpose of giving support unavailable elsewhere. There are others of us who have gone as far as to make careers of this through coaching and/or advocacy.

There are two very differing groups among those with ADHD. There are those hold it as a gift, and there are those who hold it as a disorder or even a curse. As far as who is correct, I will tell you the way I see it.

Imagine ADHD as if it were an ocean. The ocean is viewed by people differently, and it depends largely on their perspective. I suppose if someone were sitting on a sandy beach with family or friends looking out across the ocean sunset, it might appear as a gift to them. If someone is sitting on the edge of a boat while deep sea fishing with their close friends, or cutting up on some type of pleasure craft, then the ocean would seem as a wonderful and welcome part of their life.

On the other hand, if a man or woman is treading water for their sixth consecutive hour in the middle of the ocean because the ship they were on just sank, they might feel scared. If they had no means to communicate with anyone, they might feel forgotten or alone. If the corpse of a man were floating next to them and bloodying the waters, then the fear of being eaten alive may enter their minds.

It is the same ocean or the same ADHD. In the first situation, I don't imagine there are many of you would not appreciate the ocean. You would enjoy it, embrace it and perhaps long for it. You would be happy for the fact the ocean was there. No one would argue with you.

However, if a few days later, you were to find yourself in the middle of it, all alone with no sign of help or hope of survival, then the same ocean you embraced as a gift before would lose much of its appeal. Just as the ocean, ADHD can be either friend or foe, gift or curse, danger or sanctuary.

For many years, I was floating in the middle of the ocean. I felt alone, scared, and insignificant. I had no one I could talk to about the problems I had and no one who I believed could help me. It was not until I got treatment I decided I was going to be the person I wanted to be. I was tired of floating and just being a slave to the powerful ocean currents. I decided I loved Tom Nardone, and I was going to be that guy. I was sure there would be others who would love him, too.

I began to say all the things I was once afraid to say. I did all the things I once was afraid to do, and I did them in the way I wanted to do them. Not everybody liked it, but many others did. I discovered it was easier to be myself than to be in a state of constant worry about the perception of others. Today, when I hear people dealing with this problem, I usually tell them to be themselves and tell all those other people to go hump a stump.

I am Tom Nardone. I have written this because I love ADHD people, and I want them to know they are not alone in their daily life struggles. It was mainly for them I wrote these words. I did not write to promote understanding in the non-ADHD community. I have no need or desire for other people to believe or understand the trouble I have. I am quite content for the whole world to believe it is all nonsense or all in my head. Their belief in the existence of ADHD does not make it any easier for me to find my keys in the morning.

This was also for the parent of the ADHD child getting bullied on the playground for not being like the other kids. This was for the kid who studies all night and still cannot seem to understand his test questions. This was for the adults who cannot hold down a job, and this was for

ADHD people or those of you with ADHD loved ones who do not or have not yet realized what is awesome on the inside.

Whichever person you may be, I hope you found something here. If you didn't, I apologize and please don't let my shortcomings as a writer prevent you from trying to find it. I believe there is a hero living inside of you. I believe if you search for it, you will find it.

I am Tom Nardone, and you are welcome.

About the Author

By Carolyn D'Argenio

Tom Nardone is a freelance writer, blogger, and uniquely motivational speaker. He didn't intend to be any of these things. In the early days of his web design and programming career, he set out to experience "the blog" first-hand. He wrote about what he knew best: himself.

He is Tom Nardone, and he is a self-proclaimed fountain of insight. Tom's blog ADHDpeople.net has become wildly popular. Thousands of regular followers log on daily for those nuggets of sarcastic truths, inspiration, and laughter.

Ask Tom Nardone why he writes, and he will candidly admit it is for the attention. This is a typical Tom Nardone response. Funny, honest, and sticky. *Does he write for attention because he has attention deficit disorder?*

Tom Nardone was diagnosed with Attention Deficit Hyperactivity Disorder at age 29. Through his writing, he candidly shares relatable experiences of living with untreated and treated ADHD. Tom doesn't consider ADHD a curse, nor does he wish for a cure. It is precisely this attitude that has inspired countless bloggers, ADHD coaches, parents, educators, and the ADHD community.

Tom Nardone writes about ADHD to encourage people to embrace the excitement, creativity, resilience, and sensitivity characteristic of many diagnosed with ADHD. His style is infused with frankness and humor. His focus is promoting self-acceptance through entertainment.

Tom Nardone's articles have been featured in a number of online publications, including *ADD Connect, ADHD Roller Coaster: News and Essays About Adult ADHD, and Living ADDventure.* He is an active contributor to discussions on dozens of blogs, clearly establishing currency in popular ADHD culture. Tom has been a featured guest on *The Miss ADD Show, Attention Talk Radio, ADHD ReWired, and See in ADHD*

Tom Nardone and his wife of eleven years, Yvonne Nardone, who is also diagnosed with ADHD, recently launched a podcast called *The Tom Nardone Show.* They welcome listeners into their double-diagnosed lives and show what it's like to live amidst their chaos, confusion, and complete companionship. They hide nothing.

Tom Nardone writes and broadcasts from his not-so-tidy man-cave in Simpsonville, South Carolina. He does and always has make time for his listeners and readers. He would love to hear from you!

Contact Tom

Twitter	@tomnardoneshow
Web	http://thetomnardoneshow.com
	http://tomnardone.net
	http://adhdpeople.net
Facebook	https://www.facebook.com/tomchasingkites/
	https://www.facebook.com/tomnardoneshow/

37888924R00100

Made in the USA
Columbia, SC
01 December 2018